FOOD FROM MY
HEART & HOME

Mary's recipes in her new cookbook, strike the perfect balance of healthy, wholesome ingredients incorporated into delicious meals that your family will love. It will bring so much joy into every kitchen that cooks her wonderful recipes, and to every reader who shares in Mary's heartfelt stories. I can't wait to try her Sweet Potato Cheese Sauce with Pappardelle Pasta and Savory Zucchini Bread!

DR MICHELLE BRAUDE
Author of *The Food Effect Diet* & *The Food Effect Diet Vegan*
Founder of The Food Effect

Mary is an innovative recipe developer and food stylist who has a finesse for combining flavors to create interesting and delicious combinations. She is a master at what she does, and has a passion for creativity and inventiveness which is exemplified through her work. Mary's food stories are heartwarming. With her new cookbook you will be wholeheartedly welcomed into her home. Her recipes are great, I especially love the chapter ~ Pasta, Pasta, Pasta!

RAOUL MOMO
Co-Owner of the Terra Momo Restaurant Group

FOOD FROM MY
HEART & HOME

Entertaining, Recipes and
Stories from My Life

MARY ABITANTO

Portrait Photography by Nicole Guglielmo

Text and Photographs © Mary Abitanto 2020

Paperback: 978-1-951772-25-3
Hardback: 978-1-951772-26-0
E-Book: 978-1-951772-27-7

www.marioochskitchen.com

Creative Director: Mary Abitanto
Publishing Coordinator: Sharon Kizziah-Holmes, Paperback Press
Food Stylists: Mary Abitanto and Nicole Guglielmo
Food Photographers: Mary Abitanto and Nicole Guglielmo
Portrait Photographer and Photo Editor: Nicole Guglielmo www.nic-olephotography.com
Photo Editor: Pamela Grund`www.janegrecsek.com
Cover and Interior Designer: Lance Buckley www.lancebuckley.com
Photo of Lucerne, Switzerland: Sydney Abitanto
Photo of Cinque Terre, Italy: Sydney Abitanto
Photo of Barcelona, Spain: Sydney Abitanto
Hair Stylist: Leah Markscheid
Floral Designer: Patrice Cronin

For
Maggie, Sydney, and Jack

Gather and share a warm delicious meal,
linger over a hot cup of coffee,
and a slice of mom's cake.

I love you with all my heart.

Contents

FOREWORD

. . . .

Did you ever go on the amusement park ride Free Fall? It's a terrifying drop that finally comes to a screeching halt. This is how I felt when I lost my mom. You know the feeling – arms flailing, knees buckling – my faith would catch me. My steadfast, unyielding, constant faith. The ride (both literal and figurative) was unnerving.

Soon after I lost my mom, I was engaged and planning to start my life with Peter, now my husband of twenty years. The whole idea seemed daunting to me. I had to plan a wedding, pick a dress, choose a venue, the menu, flowers, etc. Although my mom wasn't by my side, my dad, my husband, and our entire family were, and it was a beautiful, unforgettable day.

Then what?

Then I had to learn how to cook and be an amazing wife. Did I mention I married an Italian? The pressure to be a great cook was on.

My favorite song, "Jump Right In," by the Zac Brown Band really played out in my life. I jumped right into cooking. My first year of marriage I was making everything from scratch while juggling working full-time and being pregnant, and soon welcomed my first baby girl, Maggie.

Cooking became a passion. I was on a journey in my kitchen and took with me everyone who came before me who taught me how to cook: Mom, Grandma, aunts, uncles, and now Dad. The journey in my kitchen is sometimes messy (with some semblance of order) and always colorful and artful.

Envision lots of burners going at one time. Two ovens in use on most days, especially during parties. The sound of country music blasting in the background and me, dancing or doing squats, to the beat of the music. That is what you would see if you peeked inside my kitchen. You would also see lots of happy faces.

On weekends, you would smell freshly baked bread or bagels warm out of the oven or the aroma from my tomato sauce or vegetable soup cooking on the stovetop. And of course, we celebrate happy hour with a charcuterie board with our family favorites: aged Gouda, aged cheddar, pepperoni, homemade dips, and lots of vegetables. Everyone gathers for a quick bite.

Food reconnects us. Food is comforting. Food reminds us of our shared heritage.

Come on a journey with me in my kitchen — it's going to be a fun ride — and at the end you'll feel a sense of empowerment in cooking for those you love, and enjoy the fruits of your labor.

A HEART FULL OF GRATITUDE

A heartfelt thank you to those of you who believed in my recipes, my story, and bought my cookbook.

Thank you to my children: Maggie, Sydney, and Jack, and husband Peter for being the best taste testers - you make life sweet and savory. I love you with all my heart!

A special thank you to my sister, Irene, who continues to be my cheerleader, encouraging me and cheering me on every step of the way. A sister is truly a forever friend.

Thank you to my dear friends and family who tested my recipes, gave great input on this book, and continue to support me. I am profoundly grateful for you.

Thank you to my friends who supported me on my cooking journey: Denise, Christie, Graham, Michelle, and Raoul. I am incredibly grateful for your kindness.

Thank you to my photographer, Nicole, without your wonderful photography and food styling, this book would have never happened! You are so talented.

Thank you to my floral designer, Patrice, who arranged the flowers so creatively for this book.

Thank you to my talented hair stylist, Leah, who styled my hair for my book signings, events, and cookbooks.

INTRODUCTION

. . . .

Food is love.

Food is life.

Food connects families, friends, and cultures.

Feeding others allows me to provide nourishment for the people I love and at the same time nurture them. *Food From My Heart And Home* was written to inspire you to gather with your friends and family. Stay awhile to have conversations of the heart while sharing a warm delicious meal. This cookbook is chock-full of healthy recipes, life stories, and beautiful eye-catching photography that I hope inspire your family gatherings.

The kitchen is the heart of my home. I think most of us feel this way. It is where everyone gathers to share light-hearted conversations and serious discussions, where everyone gets a turn to speak and be heard (and there is a difference), and from which no one leaves hungry.

My entire extended family gathers in the kitchen to celebrate the holidays: Christmas, Easter, Thanksgiving, and special occasions like birthdays, baptisms, communions, confirmations, anniversaries, and more. It's my favorite room in the house because everyone flocks to the kitchen, a place they feel cozy, welcome, and nourished!

OUR STORY

One summer night, I attended a party down the Jersey Shore. I met Peter soon after arriving and he struck up a conversation with me. He thought I looked like Sheryl Crow. I had wavy beach hair, and I have a big smile. That sparked our conversation. He was hanging with friends who to this day are still life-long friends. We grew up in the same town but had never met. The night ended and we went our separate ways.

Fast forward one year: I was working out at the gym close to my home. I was on the bike and peered over and saw who I thought was Peter. I hopped off the bike and sauntered over to him with my hair in a high messy bun and sweat streaming down my face. I said, "You are Peter, right?" He remembered me and we chatted for a few minutes. He gave me his business card to stay in touch and we said good-bye. Now, to this day I tease him that he should have taken more of an initiative to get together with me. However, I called him, and soon after we met for the third time on our first date.

That night there was torrential rain. The winds were so high and powerful that, as Peter drove to pick me up, a huge tree fell in front of his car, missing it by inches. The truth is, he almost turned around. I guess the rest is history.

The moral of the story is surpass all obstacles and good things will happen, some things are just meant to deter you, but nothing gets in the way of true love. The timing for me was perfect, as my mom become ill soon after Peter and I met. Peter came in and swooped me up.

The gravity of my heartache acted like a catalyst for our courtship. Our relationship was solidified in the midst of my deepest despair as I felt the overwhelming love from my soon-to-be husband. His compassion for my mom was heartwarming and my love for him grew exponentially. My life at that point was akin to riding a wave as it swirls you around encompassing you, as it picks up velocity, right before it crashes upon the shore — you hold your breath until you are back upon steady ground, gasping for air.

Watching Peter push my mom lovingly in the wheelchair and bring her favorite peppermint candies when we saw her gave me a glimpse into his stellar character. She loved Peter and would say it, and I too loved Peter and knew it from these precious moments that would be ingrained in my memory for a lifetime. I knew that no matter how tumultuous the waves got, I'd have Peter by my side and that his impeccable moral compass would chart the right course for my life.

OUR HOME

Welcome to my home — Casa Abitanto! Let me tell you a little bit about this cozy place we call home. Peter and I wanted to move to a house that was spacious enough to raise our two girls, Maggie and Sydney. This was the first house we looked at during our extensive search of this suburban area in New Jersey. It was a challenge to see past the colorful paints that had been spewed on the walls of this house (and the ceilings — yes, ceilings!) — bright pinks, deep cranberries, lime greens, emerald greens — to the inherent charm of the house. After looking at many other homes in the area, we came back to our first choice.

The drive to get here was down a long, windy country road that passed a large pond engulfed with beautiful trees, local farms with far-reaching green pastures and strawberry fields, apple orchards, and multiple horse stables with white picket fences. It was truly irresistible and picturesque. We settled in and this house became a home filled with love, laughter, and a lot of silliness...This was home. This was Casa Abitanto. We soon welcomed our son, Jack, and raised our three children here, and eventually painted the walls (and ceilings!) more neutral colors.

It is common to have a few extras seated around our family table, mainly our kids' friends — high school friends and college pals. In fact, we need a larger table to accommodate everyone. They fit right in and the conversation is always flowing and sparked by what is on their inquisitive minds at that moment. We are raising teenagers and a twenty-something-year old, so the topics of discussion are always varied.

We can all relate to having family include friends, especially those of you who have been transferred far from home for jobs or the military (Thank you for your service to our country!) and are displaced. We find our family among strangers and neighbors who have welcomed us into their homes. Family is where you fit, where the feeling of love is reciprocated, and where you find comfort. A gathering of friends has coalesced into family. This is the table where you sit and where your heart belongs, so when I talk about gathering with everyone you get a sense of who gathers in my kitchen.

Now for what I cook in my kitchen. First, let me give you a little background. Our heritage is mixed: Italian, Swiss (German), Irish, Albanian (Greek), Eastern European (Polish), and little bits and pieces of other cultures as well. My recipes reflect our two worlds colliding and especially our shared European heritage. I also love exploring other cultures and learning how people cook all over the world. I am fascinated by food history and tradition. My recipes are infused with tastes from different cultures, my travels, and my own healthy creative twists on dishes. I have a knack for creating flavors in meals and desserts that work in an unexpected way.

You may wonder how I became so creative in the kitchen. After my son, Jack, was diagnosed with a myriad of life threatening food allergies when he was ten months old, we as a family switched away from processed foods which may be contaminated with potential allergens and toward whole foods. Cooking was a means of survival.

At one point, he was allergic to more than forty different foods.

The allergies had reached a crescendo and I had to act swiftly to find a way to safely feed my son. It seemed like an insurmountable task, but I was not about to fail. His well-being and happiness were paramount in my search to create food he not only could eat but would also love. I was on a mission to keep Jack safe and happy and to make him feel included. Through this creative process in the kitchen of lots of trials and errors, I had developed a knack for inventiveness which carried over into all my recipes — it was my gift. But what good is a gift if you don't share it. Right?

When you eat whole foods in a wide variety, you provide yourself and your family with the most essential nutrients you need to build a strong body. These days our American culture is besieged with a myriad of diets, some of which leave us confused about what to eat and what not to eat. If you start with whole foods and add in a few sweet, albeit still somewhat healthy, treats, eating is nourishing and so delicious! With that said, we do have some processed foods in the house for easy eating. In my opinion, it's about striking a balance. Any of my recipes can be adapted to meet your individual dietary needs. Feel free to swap things out to accommodate your likes/dislikes as well.

In addition to feeding Jack and accommodating his allergies, I am also feeding my athlete, Sydney, who is a hurdler and pole vaulter. Starting our kids off with a healthy, nutritious, and satisfying breakfast is so important, and it's even more important when you know your child has such high demands on their body. That is why I decided to include a section on "Morning Glory Starters." It offers wonderful breakfast inspiration for getting breakfast on the table. Sydney and Maggie, who loves all things savory, were my inspiration for this section of the book. I hope you enjoy it — it is one of my favorites!

Food From My Heart And Home features a delicious collection of healthy recipes for your family. Learn how to make Italian classics like handmade pasta, gnocchi and cavatelli. Explore other cultures with my Spicy Moroccan Chickpea Soup and Gambas al Ajillo or make an American Classic with a healthy twist like Smoked Gouda Butternut Squash Macaroni and Cheese. Vegetarian dishes are infused throughout many of the chapters of this book.

Scrumptious desserts await you like Lavender Infused Cheesecake and my delicious spin on a Middle Eastern cookie, Date Pinwheels with Toasted Sesame Seeds, and Lemon Poppy Seed Cookies with Glaze and much more.

Learn how to create chic cheeseboards that will wow your guests with my entertaining tips for gatherings. I also share my faith journey, which for me includes volunteering at a homeless shelter in the teaching kitchen — all sprinkled with stories from my life.

So, whomever you consider your family, may you enjoy cooking for them. Sometime soon, sit down to a warm conversation over a delicious meal and be reminded of your blessings. Pull up a chair, pour a cup of coffee or tea, and (put on your glasses — me!) indulge in a book that may change the way you think about mealtime, your family dinner conversations, and your journey through life...

A THOUGHTFUL REFLECTION:
How can we savor things more?

A slice of sweet cake, a delicious meal, a conversation, the beauty of a sunset or sunrise, a cup of coffee or tea. Tune out the world. Savor the little things and appreciate the gifts in front of you at this present moment.

You will never get back this moment — **revel in it.**

WELCOME TO
CASA ABITANTO!

CHAPTER 1

Pantry Staples

A few tips to help you navigate through my recipes:

The recipes in this cookbook have been tested at least three times. I am always happy to spend part of my day doing recipe development and testing. I have a few friends who pitch in and test my recipes for me. I feel grateful that they are always excited and enthusiastic about my recipes and I appreciate their feedback. Every recipe passes through my taste testers which consist of my family, extended family, and a few neighbors.

I maintain a healthy lifestyle and develop my baking recipes using a good quality extra virgin olive oil, vegetable oil or coconut oil. However, some recipes will contain butter. I use all-purpose flour, cake flour, whole oats or ground oats in my baking. You may swap out flours with other flour substitutes and experiment. Be sure to spoon flour into the measuring cups and then level off the excess.

In my baking recipes, I use white granulated sugar, brown sugar, sugar-free maple syrup (to cut down on sugar), sweet potatoes and fruit like applesauce or dates to sweeten recipes. I do try to keep white granulated sugar relatively low, without compromising taste, of course. You can always experiment and lower the sugars even further or use a heathier substitute like organic coconut sugar. Milk is a staple in my home, but it can be swapped with almond milk.

Jack and Peter are both allergic to tree nuts, so I limit the recipes that contain nuts. With that said, feel free to add chopped nuts to my streusel topping. My son is also allergic to eggs and sesame.

My cooking recipes are healthy, incorporating fresh and seasonal produce, and limiting excess fats like butter and cream. These recipes are also adaptable to your lifestyle. For those of you who are living a vegetarian lifestyle, feel free to swap out chicken stock which is included in some recipes for vegetable stock, and swap out meat and load up on the vegetables in the recipe. There are many vegetarian options throughout this cookbook. If you are gluten-free, feel free to swap out all-purpose flour and breadcrumbs for gluten-free flours and gluten-free breadcrumbs - chickpea flour is a great gluten-free alternative.

When making handmade pasta, feel to experiment with different flours. Using all-purpose flour in lieu of double zero "00" is perfectly fine and will still produce a fabulous tasting pasta! Double zero "00" flour is more finely ground than all-purpose flour so you may notice a texture difference. In my pasta recipes, 1 serving of pasta is equal to a handful, roughly 1 cup. With that said, Jack, who is a teenager, will eat 3-4 servings in one sitting. Something to keep in mind when planning dinner.

For my cheese sauces, use cheese that you would serve on a cheeseboard. If it's an

Here is a tip on swapping out egg in recipes: You can swap out 1 egg for ¼ cup applesauce, it works great every time in baking. You will just need to bake a little longer. Also, 3 tablespoons of aquafaba (the liquid drained from canned chickpeas) is equivalent to 1 whole egg.

over processed cheese, it may compromise the taste of the recipe - something to keep in mind. Also, I highly recommend you buy chunks of Parmesan or Pecorino Romano cheeses and *freshly grate* onto pastas!

Most importantly, a well-stocked pantry will lead you to success in the kitchen. I find that having flours, sugars, and baking ingredients in close proximity to my working space, offers me more opportunities to bake for my family.

This is an essential list of items that I stock in my kitchen and pantry. There are many more items on the list, too many to name them all.

JARS

- 8-ounce food safe glass jars with lids are my go-to for shaking up salad dressings or carrying smoothies on the go.

- larger food safe glass jars with lids are great for storage: flours, sugars, chocolate chips, dried fruits, whole oats, chai seeds, flaxseeds, almonds, raisins, pumpkin seeds, and even dried pastas and rice.

- a glass olive oil dispenser is the way I store my olive oil. It's always right on my counter for easy access.

PANTRY STAPLES

- ### Baking:

  White granulated sugar
  Light brown sugar
  Organic Coconut Sugar
  Powdered sugar
  Baking soda & baking powder
  Unsweetened cocoa, milk chocolate
  Unsweetened cocoa, special dark

  Corn starch
  Molasses
  Vanilla extract
  Sugar-free maple syrup
  Honey
  Dark chocolate
  Semi-sweet chocolate chips
  Vanilla chocolate chips
  Single serve applesauce containers
  Yeast, active dry and rapid rise

- ### Flours:

  Cake flour
  Chickpea flour
  Semolina flour
  Semola flour "Rimacinata"
  All-purpose white flour
  White rice flour
  Whole wheat flour
  Double zero flour
  Almond flour

- ### Grains And Pastas:

  Rolled oats (whole oats "oatmeal")
  Whole grain breads
  Norwegian crackers
  Brown rice
  Wild rice
  Basmati rice
  Jasmine rice
  Spanish rice
  Quinoa
  Pasta
  Whole wheat pasta
  Lentil pasta
  Soba noodles
  Couscous
  Tortillas
  Bagels

- Beans:

  Canned chickpeas
  Canned white beans,
  Canned red beans
  Canned black beans
  Lentils
  Split peas
  Red kidney beans
  Dried beans

- Seeds, Nuts And Dried Fruits:

  Shredded coconut
  Flax seeds
  Chia seeds
  Salted & roasted pumpkin seeds
  Sesame seeds
  Poppy seeds
  Dried black mission figs
  Dried dates
  Dried apricot
  Dried prunes
  Cranberries
  Dark raisins
  Yellow raisins
  Almond butter
  Almonds (whole)

- Oils, Vinegars, Condiments And Seasonings:

  Extra virgin olive oil
  Coconut oil
  Vegetable oil
  Sherry vinegar
  Rice vinegar
  Red wine vinegar
  Pomegranate red wine vinegar
  Apple cider vinegar
  White vinegar

  Aged balsamic vinegar
  Non-stick spray
  Low sodium soy sauce
  Ketchup
  Mustard
  Hot sauce
  Siracha
  Hoisin sauce
  Assorted seasonings and dried herbs

- Canned, Jarred And Boxed Foods:

  Boxed almond, coconut & oat milk
  Salsa
  Tortilla chips
  Chicken, vegetable and beef stock
  Assorted olives
  Popcorn
  Rice cakes
  Artichoke hearts
  Sundried tomatoes
  Canned corn and creamed corn
  Canned crushed tomato sauce
  Jarred tomato sauce
  Tomato paste in a tube
  Salsa Verde
  Jarred red pepper dip
  Jarred eggplant dip
  Panko Italian style breadcrumbs
  White tuna in water

MY KITCHEN ESSENTIALS

- Wood pastry board
- Wood cutting board
- Cutting board for meats and poultry (dishwasher safe)
- Wood cheeseboards varying sizes
- Assorted platters

- Salad bowls
- Pizza boards
- Silver trays
- Silicone pastry mat
- Pastry cutter
- Pastry scrapper
- Spider strainer
- Tongs
- Slotted spoon
- Flat headed wooden spoon
- Wooden spoons
- Stand mixer plus attachments for mincing ham and making pasta
- Hand mixer
- High-speed blender
- Food processor
- Food mill
- Potato ricer
- Cheese grater
- Lemon zester
- Large fork for twirling pasta
- Colanders
- Large roasting pan
- Springform pan
- Stainless steel pots
- Non-stick frying pans
- Cast iron skillets
- Baking sheets
- Ceramic coated cast iron skillet with lid
- Assorted cake and pie pans
- Loaf pans
- French rolling pins
- Rolling pins
- Measuring spoons
- Measuring cups
- Chef's knife — a good investment!
- Serrated knife
- Cheese knife
- Good kitchen scissors
- Vegetable peelers
- Vegetable scrubber
- Crepe pan
- Crepe spreader
- Rubber hot plates
- Meat and candy thermometer
- Oven mitts
- Cheesecloth
- Aprons
- Fire extinguisher

I reference foodsafety.gov website for guidelines on safe internal cooking temperatures, resting times, and updates on food recalls. Always use a meat thermometer to check temperatures of poultry, pork and meat. I use an instant read thermometer.

Always use two oven mitts when handling hot food in and out of the oven. If you are frying things like my Naan use the back burners and use extra care, as the oil can splatter. Keeping them in the back is smart!

Thoughts on Fruit and Vegetables...

I buy organic fruits and vegetables especially if I eat them in bulk, like spinach/kale, mixed greens, apples, strawberries, blueberries, dates, grapes, tomatoes, potatoes. I prefer the taste of organic sweet potatoes especially in my baking recipes. I tend to shop a few days a week and buy my produce fresh - I buy conventional produce as well.

Always wash your fruits, and scrub and wash vegetables. Let them soak in a bowl of water with a tablespoon of vinegar for 5 minutes. I use apple cider vinegar. Then rinse, dry and store.

FREQUENTLY USED HERBS

- **Basil:** Italian herb
  - *Pairs well: pasta, pizza, salads, and tomato sauce*
  - *Unexpected pairing: blend into raspberry shakes or raspberry sorbet for an earthy fresh taste*

- **Dill:** Delicate, aromatic herb in the parsley family
  - *Pairs well: potatoes, salads, chicken, soups, and sour cream*
  - *Unexpected pairing: mix into cream cheese with capers and sea salt*

- **Mint:** A highly aromatic herb, widely used in Greek cooking
  - *Pairs well: salads, watermelon, and cocktails*
  - *Unexpected pairing: use in a citrus with oranges, limes, lemons and bananas for a refreshing taste*

- **Parsley:** A mild aromatic herb widely used in American cooking
  - *Pairs well: salads, marinades, chicken, meat, and fish*
  - *Unexpected pairing: Try my Savory Zucchini Bread with parsley in lieu of Cilantro*

- **Cilantro:** Related to the parsley family, pungent aromatic, citrusy herb, common in Mexican Cooking, Latin America and Indian Cooking
  - *Pairs well: soups, guacamole, salsa to curries, noodle dishes and chimichurri sauces of Argentina*
  - *Unexpected pairing: Try my Gazpacho which includes fresh cilantro!*

- **Rosemary:** Highly aromatic herb
  - *Pairs well: chicken, potatoes, and vegetables dishes*
  - *Unexpected pairing: infused into cocktails or use a pinch of dried rosemary in savory cookies*

- **Thyme:** One of my favorite herbs, an earthy, savory herb
  - *Pairs well: all dishes - chicken, pork, beans, cabbage, carrots, chicken, corn, eggplant, fish, lamb, meats, potatoes, soups, stews, winter vegetables, bread or corn stuffing*
  - *Unexpected pairing: bake into cheesecake and cakes*

- **Sage:** Mild savory herb
  - *Pairs well: chicken, cream or butter-based sauces, potatoes, gnocchi, lentils, soups, stews, and stuffing*
  - *Unexpected pairing: add to savory cakes*

If you don't have these store-bought seasonings on hand, you can make them! Feel free to experiment and use more or less of one ingredient or omit one if you don't have.

HOMEMADE ITALIAN SEASONING

2 tablespoons dried basil
2 tablespoons dried oregano
2 tablespoons dried rosemary
2 tablespoons thyme
2 tablespoons marjoram

Pulse in blender for 1 minute and store in a glass jar with lid.

HOMEMADE HERBS DE PROVENCE SEASONING

2 tablespoons dried basil
2 tablespoons dried oregano
2 tablespoons dried rosemary
2 tablespoons dried thyme
2 tablespoons dried marjoram
2 tablespoons dried lavender
2 tablespoons dried sage
2 tablespoons dried savory

Pulse in the blender for 1 minute and store in glass jar with lid.

Storing herbs like parsley and cilantro in a mason jar filled with water in your fridge will allow them to last a while. Keep basil in a plastic bag with a paper towel. It will not last as long as parsley or cilantro. Thyme, rosemary, dill, mint and sage can be stored in the vegetable drawer. Thyme and rosemary last a long time in the vegetable drawer.

CHAPTER 2

Morning Glory Starters

Spicy Avocado Toast
with Perfectly Poached Egg

SERVES 2

My kids favorite go-to breakfast! My daughters, Maggie and Sydney, cannot get enough of this combination. Maggie likes everything spicy and savory. The addition of red chili flakes, cracked black pepper, and hot sauce kicks the spicy factor up a notch.

Ingredients:

4 large eggs

Whole grain bread

1-2 avocados

Red pepper flakes

Ground sea salt

Cracked black pepper

Hot sauce

Organic orange juice

1 tablespoon apple cider or white vinegar

Optional, a good quality extra virgin olive oil

Wire mesh strainer

Medium-sized pot filled with 4-inches water

PERFECTLY POACHED EGGS:

Fill a medium-sized pot with 4-5 inches of water and bring to a boil, add in a tablespoon of vinegar. Next, crack open an egg and pour into a tiny bowl. Then gently pour the egg onto a wire mesh strainer over the sink. Some of the egg whites will drip down. Transfer the egg back into the bowl. Before adding the egg into the boiling water, stir the water first and create a swirl in the middle of the pot, then drop in the egg.

Do this with the other eggs. No more than 2 at a time. Eggs will be done in 2-3 minutes. If you don't strain the egg first, the straggly whites will end up in your water. You know you were successful if the egg stays in tact and makes an oval shape with no egg whites left behind in the water, and the yolk of the egg is runny.

After toasting the bread, cut the avocado in half and take out the pit. Scoop out the avocado and mash the avocado onto the toast with a fork. Add a drizzle of olive oil if you wish — I like it that way! Season to your liking: salt, black pepper, red pepper flakes and hot sauce, if you like it really spicy.

Place egg on top of the toast add a little more seasonings. Serve with organic orange juice and hot coffee to jump start your day. I love this breakfast after a long workout!

Waffles with Blueberry Sauce
and Rise and Shine Shake

SERVES 2

Get yourself in tip, top "shake" this morning! This shake will really wake you up and give you a jump start on your morning. Sydney, my athlete especially loves this delicious breakfast during the week. We love shakes and you can add in some extra ingredients to your shake for added health benefits and flavor: chai seeds, ground or fresh ginger, dark chocolate cocao powder just to name a few. A wonderful way to jump (in her case) start a busy week!

Rise and Shine Shake Ingredients:

YIELDS 2 SHAKES

1 ½ cups milk (or milk substitute)

2 small ripened bananas

1 tablespoon flaxseed

1 teaspoon vanilla extract

1 tablespoon freshly brewed cooled coffee

A dash of cinnamon

Optional, ground ginger

1 tablespoon almond butter

Ice cubes

8-ounce mason jars for serving

High-speed blender

MAKING THE RISE AND SHINE SHAKE:
In a high-speed blender add milk, bananas, almond butter, vanilla, flaxseeds, dash cinnamon, 1 tablespoon freshly brewed **cooled** coffee, and a few large ice cubes. Blend on high until all the ice has broken down and the texture is creamy and smooth. If too thick, add more milk. Serve with a shake of cinnamon on top.

Ginger is known for it's anti-inflammatory properties among other health benefits. I like adding it to shakes after a long workout — either freshly grated ginger or ground ginger. It will give your shake a little zing!

Waffles with Blueberry Sauce:

Blueberry Sauce (recipe follows)

1 pint fresh blueberries

2-4 organic frozen or fresh whole grain waffles

Sugar-free maple syrup

Small frying pan

Blueberry Sauce:

1 cup blueberries

1-2 tablespoons granulated sugar

½ cup water

Heat fresh blueberries in saucepan. Next, add in ½ cup water and 1-2 tablespoons sugar. Stir until it reduces and it a rich deep hue, and the berries have broken down and have become mushy. Taste it to be sure you have achieved the right balance of flavors, not too tart, not too sweet, but remember it's hot!

Once cooled, can mix into parfaits, yogurt, on ice cream, over cake or on cottage cheese, and even swirl into cream cheese. Will keep in the refrigerator for a few days.

Make fresh waffles or heat frozen waffles in a toaster, pour the Blueberry Sauce over them, and add some fresh berries and a few drizzles of sugar-free maple syrup. Serve with icy cold, Rise and Shine Shake!

Berry Good Shake
and Oatmeal Pancakes

YIELDS 6 PANCAKES

Before a track meet I make these oatmeal pancakes and this berry shake with beet juice for Sydney. We have found it gives Sydney the energy she needs to sustain her peak performance levels. You cannot beet this winning combination!

Berry Good Shake Ingredients:

YIELDS 1 SHAKE

1 cup frozen or fresh blueberries

1 cup almond milk

¼ cup beet juice (or ½ fresh beet, peeled)

2 teaspoons flaxseed

Ice cubes

Optional, ½ banana

Optional, 1 tablespoon vanilla protein powder

High-speed blender

MAKING THE BERRY GOOD SHAKE:
Combine ingredients in a high-speed blender. You will need a high-speed blender if you are using fresh beets. Blend on high until all ingredients are well combined. If it's too thick, add more milk. If it's too runny, add more ice.

Oatmeal Pancake Ingredients:

YIELDS 6 PANCAKES

1 ¾ cups whole oats, pulsed (or all-purpose flour)

1 teaspoon flaxseed

1 cup milk (or flavored almond milk)

1 teaspoon vanilla

1 teaspoon baking powder

1 large egg

2 tablespoons butter, warmed

1-2 tablespoons granulated sugar

⅛ teaspoon salt

Optional, dash of cinnamon

Optional, fresh blueberries

Non-stick frying pan

MAKING THE OATMEAL PANCAKES:
Combine 1 ¾ cups of whole oats along with flaxseed in a high-speed blender. Pulse until you have achieved a powder-like consistency.

Pour this into a bowl and rinse the blender. Then measure 1 ½ cups of the pulsed oats/flax (you will have some leftover). Whisk together the oats/flax, baking powder, and salt.

In the high-speed blender add milk, and egg and blend for 2 minutes on high until foamy. Then add in vanilla, warmed butter, sugar and flour mixture. Pulse until batter is a smooth consistency. Let it rest 10 minutes. Keep in mind, as this sits it will swell and absorb the milk, so have more milk on hand to mix in if necessary. These are a bit dense.

The extra pulsed oats/flax I will store on my counter in a glass jar for easy pancake prep.

MAKING OLD-FASHIONED FLUFFY PANCAKES:

Swap out the oats for 1 ½ cups all-purpose flour, skip the flaxseeds and follow the rest of the recipe ingredients above. These will be more like traditional fluffy pancakes. They are so good! Light and airy.

Heat a non-stick pan with olive oil and pour a small ladle full onto pan, heat on medium heat. You may add some blueberries to them as well. Cook for less than 2 minutes, then flip once they start to form bubbles. Serve with a side of Blueberry Sauce (page 23) and sugar-free maple syrup.

Beets have been known to increase athletic performance. It's a go-to veggie for those who want to reach higher performance levels.

Chic Bagel Bar

SERVES 6

Choose a bagel, add a schmear of cream cheese, we especially like the Herbed Cream Cheese made with chopped dill, capers, and salt, add some lox, or smoked salmon, and slices of cucumber and onions. This Chic Bagel Bar has something for everybody. I host our family for brunch during the holidays and my family loves this bagel bar.

Chic Bagel Bar Ingredients:

Store-bought or Easy NY Style Bagels (recipe in Chapter 7 (page 137)

1 (16 ounce) container plain cream cheese

Blueberry Cream Cheese (recipe follows)

Herbed Cream Cheese (recipe follows)

2 large oranges, cut into slices

1 English cucumber, cut into slices

1 red onion, thinly sliced

1 small bag radishes

3-4 vine tomatoes, cut a few into slices, leave some on vine

1 bag dried apricots

1 (8 ounce) package lox or smoked salmon

1 avocado, cut into slices

1 dozen eggs, soft-boil and hard-boil

Ground sea salt

Garnish: capers, fresh dill, fresh chives, fresh thyme, everything bagel seasonings

Here's some more delicious toppings and bagel bar ideas:

butter (try herbed butter)

a variety of cream cheeses (blueberry, vegetable, onion and chives)

a variety of jams (raspberry, strawberry, fig, grape)

cooked bacon (turkey or even vegan bacon)

tuna salad

egg salad

ham salad

cold cuts: turkey, ham, cheese slices

spreads: almond butter, honey, spicy mustard, hummus

greens

strawberries, sliced

Note: To make your tuna salad on the lighter side, combine it with ½ light mayo and ½ plain Greek yogurt. I like to add chopped pickles, pickle juice, onion, and sometimes celery and capers.

Lox and smoked salmon—specifically Nova salmon, the type referred to as "lox"—both have a silky, buttery texture. But true lox tastes saltier, while Nova has a smokiness to it.

Growing up I remember my mom used to mince ham and we all loved it! I recently bought the mincing attachment to my stand mixer and use it to mince ham. My family loves it with mayo, onion, celery and seasoning. Sometimes I mince it with fresh thyme.

SOFT-BOILED EGGS:

Place eggs in cold water, bring to a boil and cook for 6 minutes and place eggs in cold water to stop the cooking process. Peel once cooled and slice in half lengthwise. Add sea salt and chopped dill.

HARD-BOILED EGGS:

Place eggs in cold water, bring to a boil and cook for 10 minutes and place eggs in cold water to cool. Peel once cooled.

MAKING THE BLUEBERRY CREAM CHEESE:

Follow the recipe for Blueberry Sauce at the beginning of this chapter. It is best to refrigerate this for a few hours or overnight, then swirl in 1-2 tablespoons of the cooled blueberry sauce into about 4-5 tablespoons cream cheese.

MAKING THE HERBED CREAM CHEESE:

Add 5-6 tablespoons cream cheese into a bowl. Mix in 1-2 tablespoons chopped dill, 1 tablespoon capers and add a sprinkle of sea salt. Garnish with more dill and capers on top.

Mini SupHERpower
Healthy Muffins

YIELDS 42-45 MINI MUFFINS

These muffins were inspired by my daughter, Sydney, who will be starting college as a Division 1 Athlete right around the time this cookbook is published. Feeding an athlete takes a lot of planning and creative footwork. You want to pack in the vitamins, nutrients, protein, carbohydrates, and fats to sustain their energy and maximize their performance level, but at the same time you want to create delicious food. These muffins check all the boxes. Now you know why I call them SupHERpower Muffins! Let's continue to encourage our girls to be great athletes.

You will love these muffins. They are the most delicious muffins AND good for you!

Ingredients:

2 cups whole oats, pulse into a powder-like consistency

½ cup whole oats

½ cup all-purpose flour (or substitute almond flour or rice flour)

2 large eggs

¾ cup mashed organic yam (or sweet potato) (1 medium)

¼ cup sugar-free maple syrup

1 tablespoon flaxseed

¾ cup light brown sugar

6 pitted dried dates, soaked in hot water

6-8 fresh blackberries (or handful fresh blueberries)

1 cup extra virgin olive oil

1 teaspoon baking soda

2 teaspoons vanilla extract

1 teaspoon cinnamon

½ teaspoon ground ginger

¼ cup light sour cream

½ teaspoon dried rosemary, for a fragrant muffin

High-speed blender

Stand mixer

24 non-stick mini muffin tin

Non-stick olive oil spray

Streusel Topping:

½ cup all-purpose flour (or rice flour)

¼ cup light brown sugar

¼ cup quickly pulsed whole oats (plus a few tablespoons whole oats)

½ teaspoon cinnamon

½ stick salted butter, softened

Start by cooking the pierced yam in the microwave, cook for roughly 10 minutes or until a fork can easily pierce it. Let this cool completely. Alternatively, you may also roast the yam in the oven.

Note: choose organic yams or organic sweet potato for a more flavorful muffin. Oftentimes yams and sweet potatoes are interchangeable in the supermarket. Just be sure you choose one with deep orange skin, and deep orange flesh.

In the meantime, gather your ingredients, because there are a lot in this recipe! Well worth all the effort it takes to make these. Start by preheating the oven to 350 degrees.

Next, soak 6 pitted dried dates in hot water for 5 minutes until softened.

In the meantime, set up the blender add 2 cups of whole oats and 1 tablespoon flax-seed — pulse until they become a powder-like consistency. Add them to a bowl along with another ½ cup of whole oats (do not pulse) and ½ cup all-purpose flour, and 1 teaspoon baking soda. Whisk together these ingredients and set these aside.

In the bowl of the stand mixer, add the cooled yam and mix for a few minutes until there are no more visible lumps — about 2-3 minutes. Add in 6-8 blackberries (may substitute blueberries) and mix until all the blackberries break up into tiny pieces. After you mix this again and again, the blackberries will not be visible and the sweetness from them will be infused into the batter. If you substitute blueberries, use a small handful, equally as tasty but the blueberries will still be visible because the skin will not break down.

Next, drain the dates and add them to the stand mixer and mix for 3 minutes until all the ingredients are all fully incorporated. It's fine to have a few dates in larger chunks — this is why it's important to soak the dates, so they are soft and break apart.

Next, add in brown sugar and sugar-free maple syrup. Add these to the mixer and mix until these ingredients are incorporated. Then add in the olive oil and place mixer on low. While the mixer is moving add in the vanilla, cinnamon, ginger, eggs (one at a time), sour cream, and rosemary. The batter will be a brown earthy color.

Coat the pan with a non-stick olive oil spray so the muffins will not stick. Using a spoon, scoop up a heaping tablespoon and with another spoon fill the mini muffins to the top. These should make about 42-45 muffins.

MAKING THE STREUSEL TOPPING:

Soften the butter, add in the all-purpose flour, brown sugar, ¼ cup pulsated oats (just grind them first for a few seconds) plus a few tablespoons of whole oats and cinnamon. Mix with clean hands until this mixture is in bits and pieces.

With your hands add a small amount onto the top of every muffin. Bake in the oven for about 22-24 minutes or until the edges of the muffins are a golden brown.

Take out of oven and let cool 10 minutes. Using a butter knife loosen the side of muffin away from tin and place on a cooling rack. Repeat the process.

Sydney is a long-time pole vaulter, hurdler, and sprinter. She loves the sport. I can't wait to watch her compete at a college level. It is fun watching her reach new heights!

Nutritional Facts:

Eating dates will enrich your body with minerals like phosphorus, zinc, magnesium, calcium, potassium, and iron. Sweet potatoes are great for skin and hair. They have high level of beta-carotene. Blackberries are a powerful antioxidant and are rich in Vitamin C as well. Whole oats are one of the best whole grains. They provide a good source of fiber and will leave you feeling satiated longer. Power-up with these healthy, and nutritious foods.

My grandfather, traveled as a young man from German speaking Bern, Switzerland, to America and came through Ellis Island. Bern is the capital city of Switzerland. It is like a picturesque postcard - an idyllic backdrop with adorable castle-like cottages set along the river. It was the classic story of coming to America for a better life.

Then what?

Immigrants coming through Ellis island had to make a long journey, but it wasn't easy. Can you imagine picking up and leaving everything behind you, everything you know for the promise of a better tomorrow? The hope that you'd have a better life, maybe find a well-paying job or a lifetime spouse. And by the way, you had to learn the language too?! Boy, did they have tenacity! Although I never met either my grandfather or grandmother, both pictured here, on my mom's side of the family, I'm so grateful that my grandfather came to America and provided my mom's family with such a wonderful life.

This photo was taken by Sydney who traveled to Switzerland, and throughout Europe. She's very adventurous, just like my mom.

This is the quintessential photo of Switzerland. The beautiful rolling hills of grass amidst the mountains in the distance — so indicative of life — the peaks and the valleys.

Coffee Cake
with Blueberries and Streusel Topping

· ·

SERVES 8

This cake is a nod to my mom's side of the family. My grandfather came from German speaking Switzerland, and I believe our ancestors were originally from Germany. Coffee cake (more like a bread) was common in Germany where they used a yeast dough and combined sugar to make a sweet bread with a streusel topping.

Immigrants came from Germany to America and brought over the concept of coffee cake. Over time it was developed into more of a cake-like texture than a bread-like texture. American chefs also used coffee as an ingredient to make use of leftovers and flavor the cake– clever! The idea of coffee cake was embraced and today it's an ever-popular treat, but typically coffee is not added. The cake is to be enjoyed with a coffee, usually a morning treat, but can really be served any time of day.

Streusel is German for "sprinkle" or "strew" and refers to the popular crumbly topping consisting of butter, flour and sugar. A variety of crumb cake (known as "Streuselkuchen") contains flour, sugar, butter, cinnamon granules, and sometimes oats or nuts, which are sprinkled onto the batter before baking. Feel free to add whole oats or even pulse the oats and add some chopped nuts to the topping. You can even double the streusel topping! A glaze is another popular way to serve this cake.

My Coffee Cake with Blueberries is a healthy twist on a traditional coffee cake with the addition of sweet potatoes, olive oil, sugar-free maple syrup (to cut down on the sugar), brown sugar, and fresh blueberries. It is undeniably moist, melt-in-your-mouth, and delicious. Call your friend over for a slice of cake!

Ingredients:

1 cup mashed organic sweet potato (or yam) (1 large)

1 ¾ cups cake flour

¾ cup light brown sugar

¼ cup sugar-free maple syrup

1 teaspoon baking soda

1 teaspoon baking powder

1 teaspoon cinnamon

½ teaspoon ground ginger

1 teaspoon vanilla extract

2 heaping tablespoons mascarpone cheese

¾ cup extra virgin olive oil

1 large egg

9-inch spring form pan, buttered

1-pint fresh blueberries or frozen wild blueberries (about 2 cups)

Streusel Topping:

½ cup all-purpose flour

¼ cup light brown sugar

½ teaspoon cinnamon

¼ teaspoon ginger

½ stick butter, room temperature

Mix the streusel ingredients until you have lots of bits (granules) of the topping and it has a paste-like consistency. Mixing with hands is the way to go!

Start by washing and scrubbing a large sweet potato. Pierce it with a fork and cook in the microwave until a fork can easily pierce through it, maybe 12 minutes. Alternatively, you may bake the sweet potato for roughly 1 hour or until a fork can easily pierce through it.

Preheat the oven to 350 degrees.

Once the sweet potato is done, cut in half to let out the steam and let cool 15 minutes. Measure 1 cup and add it to the stand mixer. Mix for 2 minutes until it's smooth and no lumps remain.

Next, add brown sugar and mix. Then add in cinnamon, ginger and vanilla along with the maple syrup. Mix for 2 minutes on high. Add in mascarpone cheese and mix well until no lumps remain and batter is completely smooth. Last, incorporate egg and extra virgin olive oil. Mix on low for 2-3 minutes. Batter should be a beautiful orange color and smooth.

In a separate bowl, whisk together cake flour, baking soda, and baking powder.

Slowly, pour the flour mixture into the stand mixture while it's on. Let these ingredients mix for 2-3 minutes. Turn off stand mixer and use a spatula to scrape down the sides of the bowl (and the bottom of the bowl).

MAKING THE STREUSEL TOPPING:

Combine all-purpose flour, light brown sugar, cinnamon, ginger and butter in a bowl. You may place the butter in a microwave safe bowl and heat in the microwave for 15-20 seconds to soften it. Mix with your hands until you have created tiny bits or granules.

Rinse and dry the blueberries. Measure 2 cups. Fold in ¾ of the measured blueberries, leaving the rest for the top. Spray the springform pan with a non-stick spray. Pour the batter into the springform pan and flatten out the top. Add the rest of the blueberries to the top. Next, add on the streusel to the top of the cake.

Place in the oven for roughly 50-55 minutes. Cool for 20 minutes, then release spring from pan. Serve once completely cooled.

Enjoy with a hot cup of coffee — I especially like this alongside a creamy, rich Greek yogurt topped with my homemade Blueberry Sauce and fresh berries for a delicious and nutritious breakfast.

MAKING THE GLAZE TOPPING:

Combine powdered sugar, water (or milk) and vanilla. Mix until you have a slightly runny consistency and no lumps. Drizzle over the streusel topping.

Coffee Talk

My husband has been making the coffee in the morning for years and the aroma of it emanates upstairs and wakes me up. I love the smell of coffee. It elicits fond memories for me...

When I was in high school I can remember jumping out of bed to have some freshly brewed coffee with my dad and sharing a conversation before we started our day. Back then I was up early to work through my aerobic routines before I went to school because in the evenings, I would teach aerobics until late at night. Getting up at 5:30 am and having a hot cup of coffee with my dad made getting up early something I enjoyed.

There is something about coffee that I love! Sure, I love the taste, the aroma, the thought of it, but it's the conversations that take place over coffee that perk me up! It's also my favorite me time, and sometimes shared time with my hubby and kids in the morning before they jet off to school and work.

When life gets busy, slow down, reflect upon your day, and sip a hot cup of coffee which for me is sweetened with sugar and warmed milk. This is the way they serve it in Italy. They heat the milk and, ever since I visited Italy, I have been enjoying it this way...Take some time to enjoy your me time or shared time over a cup of coffee (or tea).

What are some conversations starters over morning coffee?

Here are a few thoughtful reflections:

1. *How can you be more impactful in your life/work?*

2. *How can you learn to change your reaction to things?*

3. *How can you remain focused on your goals?*

4. *How do you tune out social media distractions?*

5. *What kind of friend do you want to be?*

6. *How can you be more compassionate toward others?*

7. *How can you stay fit and healthy every day?*

8. *How do you find time for prayer and thoughtful reflection?*

9. *How can you encourage your creativity?*

Teaching aerobics and starting a fitness regimen at age sixteen laid the proper foundation for a lifetime of fitness. Denise Austin was one of my inspirations as a teenager. Her enthusiasm and positive attitude motivated and inspired me. Now that I am over fifty, I am still motivated by her! I find it's even more important to stay devoted to an everyday fitness regimen at this age. I will oftentimes follow her workout videos. I also do combined workouts: walking, jog, bike, Pilates, yoga, weights, stretching and hitting the speed bag!

CHAPTER 3

Entertaining Tips and Small Bites

Earthy Cheeseboard
with Mashed Blackberry
Pomegranate Spritzer

SERVES 6-8

If you are hosting a cocktail party — this platter will be one your guests will love! Be sure to make the cheeseball one day ahead. Simple and elegant entertaining at its best paired with a refreshing Mashed Blackberry Pomegranate Spritzer.

Ready, set, entertain!

Cheeseboard Ingredients:

Homemade Cheeseball (recipe follows)

1 store-bought hummus or Homemade Hummus (recipe follows)

1 bunch red grapes

Mixed pitted olives, green and Kalamata

4-5 fresh figs

1 head cauliflower (orange, purple or white)

1 (6 ounce) container fresh blackberries

1 small bag mixed carrots

1 package Norwegian Crackers

1 package rice crackers

1 package apricots

1 (7.5 ounce) package smoked Gouda slices or yellow cheddar cheese slices

1 medium round brie

1 package white cheddar cheese

1 package baby zucchinis, cut into slices

Heart shaped cookie cutter

1 medium-sized wood board

2 knives for spreading cheeses

Garnish, rosemary and thyme

Optional, mini food safe flowers and greens

Homemade Cheeseball:

1 (8 ounce) package cream cheese, softened

1 (8 ounce) package sharp cheddar cheese, room temperature

1 tablespoon port wine

½ cup roasted and salted pumpkin seeds, crushed

1-2 fresh garlic cloves

Leaves from 3 thyme sprigs

Sprinkle sea salt

High-speed blender

Rolling pin

Homemade Hummus:

1 (29 ounce) canned chickpeas, rinsed

½ lemon freshly squeezed

¼ cup good quality extra virgin olive oil

1 fresh garlic clove or 1 teaspoon minced garlic, from a jar

¼ cup water

Sea salt to taste

Optional, 2 tablespoons tahini

Garnish with a drizzle olive oil, red pepper flakes, paprika & a few crispy & whole chickpeas

Hummus is incredibly versatile. We use it in place of mayonnaise on sandwiches and wraps, and as a dip with pita and tortilla chips, as well as for dipping vegetables. My version is made without tahini.

PREPARING THE HUMMUS:

Rinse and drain the chickpeas then put them in a blender or food processor. Reserve a small handful for garnish. Add ¼ cup of extra virgin olive oil and a little sea salt. Squeeze in half of a lemon and garlic. Blend these ingredients together. Measure out about ¼ cup of water and add slowly, a little at a time, until the chickpeas are smoothly blended.

Roasted garlic is a nice addition to pesto or hummus. Cut off the top of garlic bulb, drizzle with olive oil and roast at 400 degrees for 20-25 minutes. You may use 1 roasted garlic clove in this recipe in lieu of fresh or minced garlic which in my opinion can have a sharp aftertaste in hummus. Save the rest for other recipes.

Then taste it! This is an important element to cooking. Everyone's tastes are different. You may want to add more salt or more garlic. Feel free to swirl in some tahini too.

Once it is to your liking, transfer it into a bowl, smoothing out the top.

Add the garnish: a few sprinkles of paprika, red chili flakes, a few chickpeas, and a tiny drizzle of olive oil. You can store it in the refrigerator until you are ready to serve the platter. Always keep some extra for filling up the bowl at any party, so it always looks inviting.

Alternatively, dress up any store-bought hummus with the right about of garnish and no one will ever know! Spoon the hummus inside a bowl, smear the top and all around and up the sides of the bowl, and smooth out the top.

Add your garnish same as you did above. Fan your crackers half-way around (or all the way around) the bowl and make it the focal point for any gorgeous and inviting platter.

MAKING THE CHEESEBALL:

In the high-speed blender add the softened packaged cream cheese, garlic, thyme and half of the cheddar cut into cubes. Using the agitator blend on medium for a few minutes. Add the remaining cheddar, and a sprinkle of sea salt. Last, add in the port wine. Taste it to be sure the flavors are balanced. You may want more garlic, thyme or salt. Let your palate be your guide.

Scoop out the cheese into a bowl. Chill, covered, for 30 minutes. Then shape into a ball. In the meantime, use a rolling pin to crush the pumpkin seeds in a bag or on a cutting board with a piece of parchment paper over them. Some whole ones may remain. You may refrigerate for 2 days until you are ready to use.

Note: Alternatively, when you prepare the cheeseball, omit the seeds, and place in a ramekin and bake for 10 minutes until warm. This is equally tasty smeared on crackers.

Using the slices of smoked gouda or the cheddar cheese slices, cut out hearts using a cookie cutter. You may use 2 different size cookie cutters as I did on this board. Next, cut the multi-colored carrots lengthwise to reveal the inner veins. Then cut a few of the fresh figs in half, leaving some whole. If you cannot find fresh figs, use dried figs — my brother-in-law loves these.

Cut the mini zucchinis into slices and place in a tiny mason jar to keep with that earthy vibe.

ASSEMBLING THE CHEESEBOARD:
Make the hummus a focal point, fan out the crackers all the way around or half-way. Place the cheeseball in the corner and place a cheese knife nearby. I also place the Norwegian crackers close to the cheeseball for spreading.

Assemble as you see in this photo. Everything is well-balanced in terms of colors. Be sure to face the carrot veins upward. Add the cheese hearts fanned out, and the mini hearts (if you made them) disperse throughout board. Fill in empty spots with blackberries, figs and apricots. Your guests will love this!

I have fond memories of the days when my mom and dad would host parties and have all their friends who they referred to as the "gang" over for cocktails. Entertaining was something my parents did well. The food seemed like it was in endless supply although we were told to FHB aka "family hold back" of course until guests had arrived and were fed. Above all things, I remember my pop being the bartender behind a large table mixing drinks and cocktails. He would be proud of Maggie as our bartender. Here is her Mashed Blackberry Pomegranate Spritzer.

Mashed Blackberry Pomegranate Spritzer Ingredients per glass:

6 ounces prosecco, chilled

2 tablespoons lavender syrup, chilled

5 mashed blackberries

A few drizzles pomegranate juice, chilled

Optional, rosemary sprig to stir

Mortar and pestle stick to mash the blackberries

8-ounce mason jar

Ice cubes

Muddle the blackberries in the mason jar, add ice cubes, chilled prosecco, lavender syrup, a few drizzles pomegranate juice, and add a sprig of rosemary to stir the drink. Be sure to give it a taste. Adjust ingredients according to your tastes. This drink is so delicious refreshing!

Note: There is a recipe for how to make lavender syrup under Lavender Infused Cheesecake in Cakes and Cookies Chapter (page 147). Follow those directions. Be sure to refrigerate the lavender syrup before adding it to the drinks.

Chic Cheeseboards

Cheeseboards have an assortment of cheeses paired with crackers, sometimes meats and are commonly known as a charcuterie (pronounced "shahr-ku-tuh-ree") boards. I have a fluid interpretation of a cheeseboard and will often include some vegetables on my cheeseboard along with fruit for a pop of color. Create cheeseboards/platters based on what your family and friends love to eat.

Remember we eat with our eyes too!

Here are tips to create eye-catching colorful and vibrant boards that will have that wow factor:

~ *Start with a beautiful round or rectangular shaped wood board. The color options are endless — choose a rustic or more refined board based on the occasion. You can even use a solid color platter or a silver tray depending upon the event. Entertaining outside - use a rustic board. Hosting a casual party — choose a wood board to create that casual vibe. Hosting a cocktail party — use a silver tray.*

~ *Go-to cheeses: Brie, aged Gouda, aged cheddar, cheddar, spicy cheddar, herbed goat cheese, Gruyere, and I especially love my Homemade Cheeseball (page 41) rolled in crushed roasted and salted pumpkin seeds.*

~ *Rule of thumb for a medium board: Pick 4 cheeses you like and choose a variety of soft, hard, and crumbly cheeses. Thinly slice some and use a cookie cutter to create different shapes like triangles, stars, hearts - and look for a color balance - a few white cheeses, and some orange or a colored rind. Cut some in squares, or cubes too for easy snacking. If you are serving Italian-Americans — provolone and mozzarella are a must on a board!*

~ *Go-to dips: Homemade Hummus (page 41), Red Pepper Hummus (page 61), or lemony hummus are all great options. Pick at least 2 different vegetables for dipping, and pita chips for scooping it up too.*

~ Go-to fruits: Fresh strawberries, raspberries, cantaloupe slices, mini oranges, orange slices, pomegranates, red & green grapes, red apples, mini pink lady apples and blackberries are great! Fresh Black Mission Figs cut in half — if you can find them. Be sure to cut some strawberries in half lengthwise to show their gorgeous veins.

~ Choose an assortment of dried fruits, seeds, and nuts like figs, pitted dates, apricots, roasted & salted pumpkin seeds, almonds or walnuts. Even chocolates like dark chocolate squares are great in small quantities for that salty-sweet vibe. Be mindful of nut allergies, and keep nuts separated in a bowl close by.

~ Choose an assortment of crackers like Norwegian crackers for an earthy vibe, round seeded crackers and rectangular or triangular crackers and pita chips. Fan round crackers around a round brie and place in the center of the board as a focal point. Offer fig, raspberry or strawberry jams and honey with a drizzle stick.

~ Go-to meats. Salami, prosciutto, and pepperoni are great choices — you can get creative and wrap them around breadsticks or roll with provolone cheese slices. These are must-have for any Italian-American gathering.

~ Go-to vegetables: Sugar snap peas, cucumbers, sliced peppers, multi-color petite carrots that still have the ends intact and are cut in half lengthwise, mini tomatoes, cauliflower, red radishes, watermelon radishes, broccoli, zucchini and more...

~ Display cheese knives for guests to cut cheeses. Do cut a few pieces. Labeling cheese isn't necessary but can be very charming. Leave cheeses on counter for at least an hour (or more) then cut. Sometimes I will assemble some crackers with cheese and a drizzle of honey, so guests get ideas for making cracker-cheese sandwiches.

Garnish will make the cheeseboard go from good to chic with these few tips:

Add fresh thyme & rosemary sprigs, mint leaves, pomegranates broken into pieces, loose pomegranate seeds, eucalyptus leaves around the board, food safe flowers, and opened sugar snap peas. Fan out crackers and cheeses. Garnish soft cheese with rosemary or fresh thyme. Use earthy bamboo toothpicks for easy snacking. Use matching glass or color coordinated ceramic bowls for olives, pickles, seeds, nuts, and soft cheeses.

COLOR THEMED BOARDS:

If it's fall, choose an earthy autumnal vibe with cheeses and fruits/vegetables. Choose colors in the brown and orange family and accent with greens or deep purple for a pop of color. If it's the holiday season, use greens, bright reds, white, purples and earthy tones to set an eye-catching holiday tone or do a winter themed board with white cheeses and blue fruits. For summer, go with bright, vibrant colors: reds, oranges, green, yellow. Or create a monochromatic board like all reds for Valentine's Day.

DIPS:

To make things easy when entertaining buy store-bought dip like hummus and jazz it up with lots of seasonings on top, a drizzle of olive oil and crispy chickpeas. No one will know you didn't make it.

Use eco-friendly dishes for dips and soft cheeses — lettuce or cabbage leaves can be arranged into a bowls or even use a pepper. This is creative and you don't have to get back your bowl from your sister-in-law!

Design Tips:

Start in the center of the board and create a focal point. For instance, place a hummus dip in the center of the board and start from there, building onto the board with all the cheeses. Or if you have a round brie, place that in the center of the board, and build around it.

If you have round cheese, like a brie or a bowl of hummus, fan crackers either half-way around it or all the way around it to add a bit of flare to your board.

Create rose shaped salami pieces, fold in half, then fold in half again then place upward facing. Be sure to sandwich them in tightly. Create different clusters around the board or create a salami rose river streaming through your board. Create a river of crackers too or fan them out. You can fan out cheese that are cut into rectangles or triangles — to create balance add them to both sides of the board.

GRAZING TABLE:

If you are planning a cocktail party, do a grazing table and create a large-scale cheeseboard. You can incorporate hot dishes like my Cauliflower Fritters (page 55) into it. Everyone appreciates something warm. These tips will come in handy when you are hosting your next party. Cheers!

Creamy Burrata
with Sundried Tomatoes and Basil

SERVES 4

Burrata is a creamy blend of textures coming together in one delectable bite. Its sister cheese, mozzarella, is very good too, however, burrata in my opinion, has a perfect combination of taste and texture. The outside looks like a mozzarella ball, but as you cut into it, the creamy interior is revealed — it's creamy, cheesy goodness. Burrata, meaning "buttery" in Italian is made from a mix of mozzarella and buffalo cheeses on the outside layer encasing the inner beauty made from curd and fresh cream.

Burrata is a made by cheese artisans in Southern Italy, especially in the regions of Apulia — the heel of Italy. As I would suspect, it is believed that the burrata uses the scraps from the mozzarella cheese, so as not to waste, and this may be the very reason it came into existence.

Serve it as an appetizer for your guests at your next party and this will vanish quickly! In this dish I have paired it with sundried tomatoes, fresh basil and olive oil. Use a balsamic glaze and send this dish over the top. We also really love it combined with the balsamic glaze and a light pesto sauce paired with crusty Italian bread.

Ingredients:

2 (8 ounce) containers burrata cheese

1 jar sundried tomatoes, whole

Ground sea salt

1 bunch basil, chopped and some whole

Balsamic vinegar or glaze

A good quality extra virgin olive oil

Optional, jarred pesto sauce or Homemade Pesto (recipe follows)

Small platter

Homemade Pesto:

1 cup baby spinach

1 cup baby kale

Small handful fresh basil leaves

¼ cup Parmigiano Reggiano cheese, freshly grated (or more)

1 fresh garlic clove

½ lemon freshly squeezed

Sea salt to taste

A few drizzles good quality extra virgin olive oil

Note: My favorite balsamic vinegar is an 18-year aged balsamic vinegar that tastes more like a glaze. It's very rich and thick, and pairs well with this dish.

Each container of burrata should have 2 balls, open the containers, drain the liquid and plate them. Next, rinse and dry the basil, some leaves can remain whole. Set these aside.

Open the jar of sundried tomatoes, you can use whole or julienne. Drain a few tablespoons of tomatoes and plate them next to the cheese and top with basil. Then drizzle a good quality extra virgin olive oil on the burrata and tomatoes along with some balsamic glaze.

If you made the pesto as an added layer of flavor, add that as well. Don't forget a good sprinkle of sea salt! Sometimes we add some fresh avocado — the flavors pair well together.

MAKING THE PESTO:

Combine kale, spinach, basil, garlic, olive oil, cheese, ground sea salt, and a squeeze of lemon. Blend until the texture is creamy. Be sure to taste it and adjust it according to your preferences. If you want it saltier, add more cheese and sprinkle more sea salt. Using Parmigiano Reggiano will impart a great flavor into this pesto, but Parmesan cheese is also a good choice. Double or triple this recipe if you want to make pesto pasta.

Burrata pairs well with fresh or grilled peaches, strawberries, or beets. Add to pizzas or pasta dishes. There are many possibilities with this delicate, rich and creamy cheese!

Cauliflower Fritters

YIELDS 10 FRITTERS

Make these and the kids come running to the kitchen! They are reminiscent of Italian rice balls without being deep fried. Everyone is substituting riced cauliflower for rice, so I thought this was a creative and healthy twist on an Italian classic. These are baked first and then quickly fried in a little oil. My Cauliflower Fritters are crispy, gooey, and delicious all in one crunchy bite. The only problem you may experience with these is that they will vanish too fast, so double my recipe or, better yet, triple it! This recipe will yield about 10 medium-sized fritters. You can serve these as an appetizer or alongside your dinner. These are great for entertaining.

Ingredients:

1 (10 ounce) bag seasoned frozen cauliflower florets "ranch or garlic", cooked

1 ⅓ cups all-purpose flour

⅓ cup shredded mozzarella cheese

1 tablespoon herbed spreadable cheese

1 cup milk

1 box panko Italian style breadcrumbs

Seasonings: salt, pepper, dried parsley, and paprika

A good quality extra virgin olive oil

Non-stick spray and non-stick pan

Optional, chives

Sour Cream Dip:

⅓ cup sour cream

2 tablespoons herbed spreadable cheese

A few things to keep in mind before you start:

- When you shape the balls, roll them in the palms of your hands, dip in flour then milk, and then add breadcrumbs to a tiny bowl and roll it all around the edges of the bowl.

- You may dip in egg instead of milk.

- Season, season and season! This will greatly impact the taste.

- For easy eating, pipe the dip onto fritters and place them in a mini cupcake holder.

Start by heating the cauliflower in the microwave according to the directions on the bag. Let it cool, then drain it and press out the moisture. Place in a bowl and add in the herbed spreadable cheese, ⅓ cup of all-purpose flour (reserve 1 cup for dipping) and mozzarella cheese and mix these ingredients together. If you find it's still a little wet add in a tablespoon or more of flour and mix again.

Add in black pepper, sea salt, and a hint of paprika. Shape into balls. These can also be shaped into tiny footballs as an appetizer during football season.

Set up three bowls:

1 bowl with ½ cup all-purpose flour

1 bowl with ½ cup of Panko breadcrumbs

1 bowl with ½ cup milk

Reserve the rest of the ingredients to use as needed. Season the flour with salt, black pepper, and paprika. Season the panko breadcrumbs with the same seasonings and a sprinkle of dried parsley as well. Add in a good amount of paprika so these turn deep brown.

START THE DIPPING PROCESS:

Dip each ball in flour, then milk, and last in the breadcrumb mixture. Roll them around the edges of the bowl to coat the entire ball. Place on a cookie sheet lined with parchment paper. Spray the fritters with non-stick spray to ensure they get crispy on the outside. This is an important step!

Preheat the oven to 375 degrees. Once it is heated, place these in the oven for about 18 minutes. The last 2-3 minutes I crank up the heat to 400 degrees.

Set up a non-stick frying pan and cover the bottom of the pan with a few drizzles of olive oil. Heat on high heat and place the balls in the olive oil and brown all over, turning on all sides. Cook for about 4-5 minutes or until they are browned and crispy! Place on a plate lined with a paper towels to absorb excess oil.

MAKING THE SOUR CREAM DIP:

Combine sour cream and herbed spreadable cheese and mix using a hand mixer to create a smooth texture. Place inside a plastic bag and snip off the end. Place a dollop on each ball and place inside a mini cupcake holder for easy eating.

Alternatively, if you make these into footballs, create the lace effect on top by piping with dip, and place on a serving tray with fresh chives to mimic the turf. You will score a touchdown with these! These are still good next day, just heat a few seconds in the microwave.

Fig and Cheese Crackers

YIELDS 24 CRACKERS

In the summer, my Dad and I would go to the local farmer's market while vacationing at the beach, where we owned a family home. We would buy fresh Black Mission figs - it was a summer tradition for us. To this day, I think of my dad whenever I eat a fig. He would really like this combination using fresh figs. It's a savory and sweet combination with the creamy cheese alongside the salty prosciutto and sweet figs.

Ingredients:

2 tablespoons crème fraîche

6 tablespoons crumbled goat cheese

A drizzle of honey

5-6 thyme sprigs

Sprinkle dried thyme leaves

24 buttery, salty crackers

10 small fresh Black Mission figs cut into slivers, stem off

3 slices smoked prosciutto

Preheat oven to 400 degrees

Cut the figs into quarters. You want them to have a bite to them, but not so big they overpower the cracker.

Next, mix the crème fraîche and crumbled goat cheese with a hand mixer. It should be lumpy - the lumps will melt once you bake it. Place a dollop about 1 teaspoonful onto each cracker, add a drop of honey to the cheese, and a sprinkle of dried thyme.

Last add a sliver of fresh fig, and tiny piece of prosciutto to the side of fig attaching to the cheese so it sticks. Top off with a tiny piece of fresh thyme for aromatics and flavor. You may drizzle more honey if you wish.

Bake at 400 degrees for 7-8 minutes and serve warm right out of the oven.

Gambas al Ajillo
(Garlic Shrimp)

. . . .

SERVES 6-8

On the weekends, my husband and I visit our favorite local Spanish restaurant for happy hour and order Gambas al Ajillo. We love the taste, and the price is good too, since it is a happy hour special. I did a little research and experimented with a few different Spanish garlic shrimp recipes, some had brandy in them and lemon or lemon zest. I finally settled on this recipe and absolutely love it! When our extended family comes over, I serve it and they devour it.

This dish is very aromatic, and flavorful and has a spicy kick. The herbed garlicy butter creates a great flavor base for this classic Spanish shrimp dish. It is very Spanish to add sherry to dishes which will give it a bit of a tangy taste. The crusty bread for dipping is a must. Alternatively, feel free to use the same recipe and toss with angel hair pasta and serve for dinner or pair with green beans for a lighter meal.

Ingredients:

1 ½ pounds shelled and deveined extra-large fresh shrimp, tails intact

5-6 fresh garlic cloves, finely diced

½ cup good quality extra-virgin olive oil

½ cup fresh parsley, finely chopped

2 tablespoons sherry vinegar

½ teaspoon or more red pepper flakes

4 tablespoons salted butter

Ground sea salt

Dried parsley flakes

1 loaf Italian bread, sliced

Optional, 3 tablespoons pimentos

Ceramic coated cast iron skillet or non-stick pan

. . . .

In a large bowl, toss fresh shrimp with a sprinkle of ground sea salt and let stand for 10 minutes.

Note: If you can find Argentinian red shrimp try them. They are sweeter than regular shrimp and have a texture and taste more like lobster. They are incredibly good! They cook in half the time as regular shrimp. You'll know when they are done if they curl up and are opaque on the inside. They are naturally pink, so do not go by the color with this type of shrimp.

In the meantime, preheat the oven to 425 degrees. Cut the Italian bread into ¾ inch slices and place on a baking sheet. Heat in oven for 7-8 minutes until crusty and golden brown. Take out of oven, add a drizzle of olive oil and a sprinkle of dried parsley flakes and sea salt. Set these aside.

In a medium-sized ceramic coated cast-iron skillet, combine the butter, and olive oil and cook over medium-low heat and add garlic, stirring occasionally, until the garlic is translucent about 8 minutes. Add ½ teaspoon of red pepper flakes and cook, stirring, until everything is very aromatic.

I leave the tails on the shrimp for easy eating. Add the shrimp to the skillet and cook over medium-low heat, stirring and turning the shrimp occasionally, until barely pink, about 4-5 minutes. Take off heat while still slightly pink, add in 2 tablespoons of sherry and stir to incorporate all the flavors.

Stir in the finely chopped parsley and more red pepper flakes and a generous pinch of sea salt. Let stand until the shrimp are cooked through (no longer pink in the center), 5 minutes. Always check for doneness by cutting through 1 or 2 shrimp.

You can place the bread back in the oven for 2 minutes while the shrimp are resting. Serve the shrimp in the skillet with crusty bread for dipping. Enjoy!

Rainbow Crudité

SERVES 8

This crudité (pronounced "kroo-di-tey") is visually appealing, vibrant, and healthy way to entertain your guests. It is an easy assembly as well. Make a few hours in advance and store covered in the refrigerator. You can even prepare this 1 day ahead. I avoid using the mini carrots which have a white film on them and can look messy. Be sure to open some of the sugar snap peas to reveal the peas inside. Also, if you can find zucchini flowers, add them to the board as well for an organic, earthy vibe.

Ingredients:

1 red pepper, rinsed, seeded, and thinly sliced

2 yellow peppers, rinsed, seeded, and thinly sliced

1 orange pepper, rinsed, seeded, and thinly sliced

1 large box mini tomatoes

1 (16 ounce) bag mixed petite colored carrots, cut in half lengthwise

1 bag celery, rinsed, peeled, and thinly sliced

1 medium zucchini, rinsed, peeled, and thinly sliced

1 small bag sugar snap peas

Red Pepper Hummus (recipe follows)

Garnish: fresh thyme sprigs, sugar snap peas opened

Large wood tray, something with sides so the veggie can rest on it.

Line wood tray with parchment paper

Red Pepper Hummus:

1 cup canned chickpeas, rinsed

1 red pepper, roasted

2 fresh garlic cloves, whole

½-1 shallot, roasted

Ground sea salt to taste

A good quality extra virgin olive oil

Red pepper flakes

Garnish: paprika, red pepper flakes, and chickpeas

High-speed blender

MAKING THE RED PEPPER HUMMUS:

Preheat oven to 425 degrees.

Place 1 red pepper (stems intact) and ½ shallot onto a baking sheet lined with parchment paper. Drizzle with olive oil. Place in the oven for 30-35 minutes. Do not char peppers. Once done, hold the pepper by the stem and peel off skin. Rinse out seeds, and pat dry. Let cool completely.

Next, place roasted pepper inside a high-speed blender along with chickpeas, shallot, garlic, a good drizzle olive oil. Pulse for 1-2 minutes until puréed. Add sea salt to taste, and red pepper flakes. Pulse until smooth and creamy.

Cut vegetables and assemble as you see in this photo or any way you wish. Don't forget to garnish with fresh thyme and to open some of the sugar snap peas. Show-stopper crudité!

CHAPTER 4

Soups and Salads

Gazpacho

Spicy Moroccan Chickpea Soup

Cucumber Melon Chilled Soup

Chunky Vegetable Soup

Superfoods Salad with Gigli Pasta

Cucumber Pomegranate Salad

Sweet Potato Salad

Barcelona, Spain

Gazpacho
(Summertime)

. . . .

SERVES 6

Cherry gazpacho, green gazpacho, watermelon gazpacho - the list goes on and on as to the various combinations you can create with this silky smooth and delicious chilled soup. One thing is certain is that the concept of this soup originated from Andalusia in Southern Spain where it tends to be hot. I was blessed to be able to visit this beautiful region and taste this mouthwatering, refreshing Spanish classic myself.

This authentic recipe calls for the ripest and juiciest tomatoes, day old bread, fresh garlic, a small Cubanelle pepper, onion, and the secret ingredient is the sherry vinegar. The key is to combine these ingredients and soak them for at least 2 hours (or even longer), so the flavors meld together. Then purée (twice) until you achieve a creamy, silky, smooth texture and strain (twice) through a fine sieve (or food mill) for a lighter, more elegant version of this Spanish classic. I highly recommend doing this process twice for a silky, velvety smooth and refreshing soup!

If you can find sherry vinegar from this region of Spain, even better! I used an aged sherry vinegar from California which had hints of apricot in it. I paired it with some pomegranate infused red wine vinegar (or you can use red wine vinegar) and pomegranate juice to impart extra flavor and give this soup a brighter color with more reds. I love fresh cilantro because it has such a refreshing taste, so I chose to add it into this recipe at the very end and quickly pulse it until the cilantro was broken into bits.

Ingredients:

2 lbs. ripe tomatoes, cored and chopped

1 or 2 fresh garlic cloves, chopped

1 small Cubanelle pepper (green),
seeded and chopped

⅓ cup red onion, diced

¼ cup good quality extra virgin olive oil

⅛ cup aged sherry vinegar

⅛ cup pomegranate infused red wine vinegar

2 tablespoons pomegranate juice

6 celery stalks, cut into 2 ½-inch pieces

1 ½ cups day old rustic white or
Italian bread, no crust

Ground sea salt & black pepper, generous amount

1 cup fresh cilantro (or parsley), loosely packed

Garnish: chopped tomatoes, chopped cilantro
or swirl of either sour cream or crème fraîche

Large bowl with tight-fitting lid

Food mill

Pairs well with crab meat as a topping
and rustic bread for dipping

6 small bowls

First, you'll need a large bowl with a tight-fitting lid to store this soup in the refrigerator for a few hours, the longer the better!

Start by cutting the tomatoes, core and chop them. This is a seasonal soup, so be sure you are choosing the freshest tomatoes possible. Organic is a great choice. After a long, hot day on the beach, I would make this soup with my tomatoes that are ripe on the vine. Save a little chunk of tomato for garnish.

Next, cut the Cubanelle pepper in half, rinse the seeds, and chop. Dice the red onion. You may use Vidalia onion, but I prefer the taste of the red onion for this soup and the color enhances the color of this soup. Chop the garlic as well.

If you have day old rustic Italian bread use this. Cut off the crust and dice into cubes. Use roughly 1 ½ cups of bread. It will expand once you soak it, so you don't need a lot. Fresh Italian bread works too, but historically this soup was made with day old bread, as to not waste!

In the bowl, combine the tomatoes, pepper, garlic, red onion, olive oil, pomegranate juice, pomegranate infused red wine vinegar, aged sherry vinegar, and a good sprinkle of ground sea salt and black pepper. Let this soak for at least 2 hours.

After 2 hours (or more), blend all the ingredients in a high-speed blender on high — 3 minutes until smooth. Strain the mixture through a strainer or a food mill, pushing all the liquid through with the back of a wood spoon. Discard the solids. Repeat the blending and straining process twice for an exceptionally velvety smooth soup!

Don't forget to pulse the cilantro in at the very end to break it into bits.

Make a cute celery spoon for eating this yummy soup! Cut celery into a 2 ½-inch chunk, closest to the stem, round out corners, and use for spoons.

This soup will last for up to 2 days in the refrigerator. This is probably one of my favorite recipes and although it doesn't make a lot — the taste is so smooth and refreshing. It will take you to Spain in one tiny sip. Great for a hot summer's day!

Spicy Moroccan
Chickpea Soup

· ·

SERVES 4

There is a long history of colonizers and immigrants who set their roots down in Morocco. As a result of these influences, there are a combination of languages: Arabic, Moroccan Arabic, Berber, and French. These influences also created a diverse cuisine in Morocco. The Berbers were known for tagine (stew) and couscous, still common in Moroccan cooking. The Arabs brought spices like cinnamon, ginger, paprika, cumin and turmeric, as well as nuts and fruits. The Moors introduced olives, and the French culture introduced delicious rich pastries. It is a blend of tastes that come together in one bite, and the rest is delicious history!

I have incorporated some Moroccan influences into this delicious and nutritious Spicy Moroccan Chickpea Soup. It has a kick with the addition of cayenne pepper. I hope you enjoy it as much as my family does!

Ingredients:

1 cup crushed tomato sauce

1 red pepper in a jar or 1 roasted pepper

½ medium Vidalia onion

4-5 carrots, slice in half lengthwise and chopped

2 (29 ounce) cans chickpeas, rinsed

1 (32 ounce) container vegetable broth

2 fresh garlic cloves, thinly sliced

1 handful fresh cilantro, bundled together and tied

3-4 tablespoons tomato paste

1 ½ cups cooked couscous

2 teaspoons aged sherry vinegar

Salt & pepper to taste

1 teaspoon paprika

1 teaspoon turmeric

⅛ teaspoon ginger

A good quality extra virgin olive oil

A pinch of cayenne pepper and red pepper flakes

Non-stick frying pan

Large pot

Garnish: crunchy roasted chickpeas, dollop sour cream

· ·

Start by peeling the carrots, cutting them in half lengthwise and adding to a medium-sized frying pan with olive oil, flat side down. Add a sprinkle of sea salt. Let this cook on each side about 5-6 minutes. They will be slightly browned. Take out of pan once done. Set aside.

Open 2 large cans chickpeas. Rinse well and drain. The juices will add a film to your soup. You will need 1 can and half of the other can. Reserve the rest. Place these in a bowl with a drizzle of olive oil, sea salt, and a few dashes of paprika and turmeric to impart added flavor. Mix well. Set these aside.

Next, take out a whole red pepper from the jar and pat dry, add it to the blender along with 1 cup of crushed tomato sauce, a tiny chunk of onion (keep the rest for dicing), a 5-inch piece of cooked carrot, 2 teaspoons of sherry vinegar, and 2-3 tablespoons of the marinated chickpeas. Purée for 1-2 minutes until smooth. You may add in a splash of vegetable stock as well if you feel it's too thick.

Add a drizzle of olive oil into the large pot and add in the remaining diced onion. Thinly slice the garlic and add that as well. Keep these on low heat for 5-6 minutes. Do not brown.

Next, add the broth to the pot, and the marinated chickpeas. Tie up the cilantro using cooking string and toss in the pan. Let this cook roughly 15 minutes. Once it comes to a boil, keep on low and simmer.

Pull out the cilantro. Do not discard.

Add in the tomato-red pepper purée and mix well. Cut the carrots into bite-sized chunks. Add a drizzle of olive oil.

Now add in your seasonings.

I use the following: 1 teaspoon black pepper, a heavy sprinkle of sea salt, ½-1 teaspoon turmeric to enhance the color and boost the health benefits, ½-1 teaspoon paprika, ⅛ teaspoon ginger, and a tiny hint of the following:

red pepper flakes & cayenne pepper which will take this soup up a notch in terms of flavor and the spicy factor. Adjust these ingredients according to your preferences.

Last, I add 3-4 tablespoons tomato paste and mix. Then add cilantro back to pot and simmer on low heat for 20 minutes. The longer it cooks the more the liquid will evaporate so have an extra container of vegetable broth on hand.

Prepare your couscous according to directions on the box. Add a few spoonfuls to each bowl. You may add some crunchy roasted chickpeas as a garnish and a dollop of sour cream to calm down the spice. Serve with my homemade Naan. Enjoy!

Cucumber Melon Chilled Soup

(Summertime)

SERVES 4

This is a refreshingly light and creamy soup. It has a similar vibe as the gazpacho but is sweeter with the addition of cantaloupe. It is a beautiful eye-catching soup, great to serve at a small gathering or luncheon. The gorgeous colors celebrate the vibrant herbs, fruits, and vegetables we enjoy all summer long.

Ingredients:

1 small cantaloupe (peeled, seeded)

1 ¼ English cucumbers (peeled, seeded)

3-4 fresh mint leaves

3 tablespoons fresh cilantro, chopped

1 ½ tablespoons aged sherry vinegar (with apricot)

1 ½ limes freshly squeezed

Ground sea salt

Tiny drizzle of a good quality extra virgin olive oil

Food mill

Garnish: watercress, fresh chives, and sour cream

Cut the cantaloupe in half and remove seeds. Cut into slivers and peel skin. Then chop it into chunks. Peel the cucumber and chop into chunks. Add these to a high-speed blender along with a drizzle of olive oil and 1 ½ tablespoons sherry vinegar. The vinegar I used in this recipe had some apricot juice in it. If you cannot find aged sherry vinegar with apricot, add a squeeze of a half of fresh peach or half of fresh apricot. Add the mint now as well, and a squeeze of 1 and half limes.

Purée this until smooth about 3 minutes on high. Add in a few sprinkles of ground sea salt. Once it's a smooth texture, add in the cilantro and pulse until it breaks it into tiny bits.

Next, strain the mixture through a strainer or a food mill, pushing all the liquid through with the back of a wooden spoon. Discard solids. Do this process twice to make it extra smooth and velvety.

Refrigerate a few hours and serve. Garnish with watercress and fresh chives. Add a dollop of sour cream. Enjoy!

Chunky Vegetable Soup

SERVES 4

You can pull this delicious, hearty soup together quickly for dinner. Use what you have on hand. I incorporated the vegetables I had in the refrigerator, and pantry staples like stock, and canned tomato sauce. My Chunky Vegetable Soup is loaded with vegetables like swiss chard, kale, carrots, and onions. I used a fusilli bucati pasta, but feel free to use any pasta or a combination of pastas and use up those half empty boxes. Great weeknight meal for a weekly veggie round up and pantry pull. Serve this on a cold winter's night served with rustic Italian bread.

This soup reminds us to eat in a rainbow of colors.

Ingredients:

3-4 large carrots

½ sweet yellow onion, diced

1 shallot, diced

½ red onion, diced

2 fresh garlic cloves, minced

1½-2 cups dry pasta, like fusilli bucati

1 (32 ounce) container chicken stock (or vegetable stock)

1 (28 ounce) can crushed tomato sauce with basil

4 swiss chard leaves, cut into ribbons (can use stems)

1 cup kale, chopped (discard stems)

1 bunch fresh thyme, bundled together

A dash of turmeric

A good quality extra virgin olive oil

Red pepper flakes, cracked black pepper and pink Himalayan salt

Optional, cream

Garnish: swiss chard ribbons, swirl sour cream, freshly grated Pecorino Romano

Ceramic covered cast iron skillet

Kitchen string

Start by adding a few drizzles of olive oil to the pan. Using a lemon grater, grate the garlic cloves into the pan. Stir for a few minutes, be sure the garlic doesn't burn. Heat until translucent.

Cook 2 cups of pasta according to box directions.

Wash, dry and peel the carrots and cut in half lengthwise and in half again lengthwise.

Then chop into bite-sized pieces. Dice the onions. Add the carrots and onions to the pan. Let this simmer on low heat for a 5-6 minutes. Add in a few sprinkles of pink Himalayan salt, cracked black pepper and a dash of red pepper flakes. Last, add in a dash of turmeric.

Next, add about ¾ container of broth and let it simmer on medium heat. Reserve the rest. In the meantime, rinse and dry the kale and the Swiss chard. Cut the swiss chard into ribbons and chop the kale. Add these to the pot. Tie up the bunch of thyme (a small handful is enough) and add to the pan. This will infuse the flavor into your soup without getting the sprigs (or sticks) in your soup.

Open the tomato sauce and add in half the can. Add in the pasta. Keep on medium heat.

As it cooks, the pasta will absorb the liquid, so you may add more tomato sauce or stock. Let this simmer about 1 hour.

Serve with freshly cut swiss chard ribbons on top and a swirl of sour cream or a swirl fresh cream, and fresh bread on the side. Enjoy!

Superfoods Salad
with Gigli Pasta

SERVES 8

This salad has cauliflower, broccoli, zucchini, onions, mushrooms, pumpkin seeds, garlic, and turmeric. My Homemade Italian Dressing pairs well with this delicious and healthy salad. I know you will love the combination.

Serve this salad for a party, or Sunday brunch. It requires time to roast the garlic, chop all the vegetables and prepare the dressing which should be added to the vegetables for roughly 1 hour so flavors can meld together. Then you can chill the salad for 1 hour before serving – so plan accordingly. Roast a garlic bulb 1 day ahead, so it's cold when you make your dressing. All your friends will want this recipe!

I use a fancy shaped pasta – gigli or campanelle, which means bell flower or little bells. The pasta resembles a bell with ruffled edges. If you cannot find it, you can do a hearty fusilli bucati – not a regular fusilli because they may break apart with the tossing of this salad. You want a pasta that is firm enough to toss around in the bowl. Even the gigli is delicate – don't over stir. Also, you do not want a pasta that the next day will be too tough to eat like penne.

Ingredients:

¾ (1 lb.) bag gigli or campanelle pasta or fusilli bucati

4 cups broccoli, chopped (1 medium)

4 cups cauliflower, cored and chopped (1 medium)

2 cups baby bella mushrooms, chopped

1 red onion, diced

3 cups zucchini, diced into cubes (1 medium)

1 bunch fresh basil

A good quality extra virgin olive oil

Seasonings: red pepper flakes, cracker peppercorn, Italian seasonings, ground sea salt, and garlic powder

Optional, 1 cup provolone cheese cut into cubes, roasted and salted pumpkin seeds

HOMEMADE ITALIAN DRESSING:

½ cup good quality extra virgin olive oil

½ cup pomegranate infused red wine vinegar

3-4 tablespoons water

3-4 fresh garlic cloves, roasted

3 fresh basil leaves

1 slice large Vidalia onion

Italian seasonings

Turmeric

Ground sea salt

8-ounce mason jar with lid

High-speed blender

Start this recipe by making the dressing. Once it is made place it in the fridge while you gather and chop all the vegetables. Ideally, you will have prepared the roasted garlic the day before — the flavor from the garlic sends this dressing over the top. Otherwise, use fresh garlic cloves.

In high-speed blender combine olive oil, pomegranate infused red wine vinegar, water, onion, a few dashes Italian seasonings, turmeric and sea salt. Squeeze out 4 garlic cloves from the roasted garlic bulb and blend on high for 2 minutes. Add the basil leaves in the last few seconds to break up into tiny bits. It should be completely puréed and smooth. Be sure to taste it. You will likely need more salt, seasonings, or garlic. Season to your liking. Store in an 8-ounce mason jar with a fitted lid in fridge while you chop vegetables.

Note: If you can find pomegranate infused red wine vinegar that is great! We are maximizing the healthy benefits with this salad, and pomegranates have many good health benefits.

Next, I chop each vegetable into bite-sized pieces. Then measure out 4 cups of each vegetable and add to a bowl. Chop broccoli omitting any stems, chop cauliflower, mushrooms and set these aside in a large bowl. Dice the zucchini into tiny bite-sized cubes. Dice the red onion as well. Set aside a tiny handful of zucchini, red onions, and basil strips for garnish - do not marinate those, save for garnish!

Note: If you can find a purple cauliflower that would make this salad even more vibrant.

Make the basil ribbons by stacking the basil, rolling them and cutting thin strips and add to the bowl with the vegetables.

Combine all the vegetables and add in half of the dressing. Be sure to shake it before you pour it. Cover and place in fridge for 2 hours so flavors meld together.

After 2 hours prepare your pasta according to box directions. You will only need roughly ¾ of the box, the star of this salad are the superfood vegetables! Bring water to a boil, and generously salt water. Once pasta is done, drain pasta in a colander.

Transfer the pasta to a large bowl and add a good drizzle of olive oil. Flavor the pasta with some seasonings. Add in a dash of the following: red pepper flakes, Italian seasonings, cracked peppercorn, a tiny dash of garlic powder, and sea salt. Mix and taste it! Let pasta cool 20 minutes.

Next, add the marinated vegetables to the cooled pasta and mix in a few tablespoons of remaining dressing. Refrigerate for a 1 hour or more before serving, or you may serve at room temperature as well.

Right before serving add garnish: reserved zucchini, red onion and basil ribbons. Toss with remaining dressing! Fish out a few of the pasta pieces to leave on the top of salad so everyone knows it is a pasta salad! Taste, taste, taste! Cold pasta salads need more seasonings than warm.

You may add in some provolone cheese before serving. Leave some pumpkin seeds in a bowl alongside this salad for topping. Enjoy!

Cucumber Pomegranate Salad

SERVES 8

This Cucumber Pomegranate Salad is a delicious and refreshing salad for the spring or summer months as well as a wonderful accompaniment to a hamburger or veggie burger. I love this salad for the following reasons: easy to prep ahead, visually appealing, a show-stopper, healthy, tasty and won't spoil in the heat!

If you are bringing to a picnic, I would skip the cheese. When you add the pumpkin seeds, do so the last minute before serving, so they remain crisp. Be sure to pick up salted and roasted pumpkin seeds. Adding a few sprinkles of pink Himalayan salt to this salad is highly recommended before you add the dressing. Feel free to the keep dressing on the side for guests to add themselves or toss the salad with dressing upon serving.

Ingredients:

3 English cucumbers, thinly sliced

1 pomegranate, cut in half

1 medium red onion, cut into thin slivers

3 tablespoons salted and roasted pumpkin seeds

1 bunch fresh dill, chop

Pink Himalayan salt & black pepper

Optional, feta cheese crumbles

Optional, 3 watermelon radishes, thinly sliced (recommended)

Pomegranate Salad Dressing:

A drizzle of a good quality extra virgin olive oil

2 tablespoons red wine vinegar

A drizzle agave syrup or honey

A sprinkle pink Himalayan salt

A dash of black pepper

Sprinkle dried basil and dried oregano

2 tablespoons pomegranate juice

1 tablespoon pomegranate seeds

A pinch of chopped fresh dill

A tablespoon finely diced red onions or shallots

Optional, a drizzle of Rosé wine

Mason jar with lid

Start by cutting the pomegranate in half. Squeeze out some juice from each half and save for salad dressing — about 2 tablespoons. Then soak the pomegranate halves in a bowl of water and break apart the flesh and the seeds will come right out and sink to the bottom. Drain in a colander. Pick out all the white pulp. Set aside the seeds.

Next, rinse and dry the cucumbers. Cut off the skin if you wish or keep some skin intact to create a design along the edges. The English cucumber's skin is not tough. You will need a good chef's knife to cut the cucumber into paper thin slices.

Now, slice the onion into very thin slivers as seen in this photo. You will need roughly 1 cup of onions. You don't want the onions to over-power this salad.

Chop a small handful of fresh dill, discard the stems. Using a large white bowl (so the colors pop) add the cucumbers and red onions, and gently toss until everything is well incorporated.

Next, add in the chopped dill, and then the pomegranate seeds (save some seeds for dressing). Add in roughly 3 tablespoons of pumpkin seeds. A handful of crumbled goat or feta cheese is a nice addition as well. You can even try some fresh creamy burrata chunks. Adding thinly sliced watermelon radishes is highly recommended so you have a gorgeous eye-catching salad.

This salad is so yummy and beautiful with all the vibrant colors! I hope it is a big hit at your next party. Add all the salad dressing ingredients to a mason jar with lid and shake well right before serving.

Sweet Potato Salad

SERVES 6-8

I love salads and enjoy eating them for lunch and sometimes dinner, but for dinner I add some type of protein like roasted chicken, or salmon, paired with the warmed sweet potatoes. It is very satisfying to me and ultra-healthy. This salad knocks it out of the park in terms of vitamins and nutrients and the colors are so gorgeous and vibrant — almost too pretty to eat!

Ingredients:

2 sweet potatoes (or yams), peeled, cut into bite-sized chunks, and roasted

1 bunch swiss chard

5-6 red radishes, thinly cut and a few whole

1 pomegranate, extract the seeds and juice

2 avocados, cut into slices

½ red onion, cut into thin slivers

1 large box arugula or baby kale (or a combination of the two)

A handful salted and roasted pumpkin seeds

A handful dried cranberries

A large wooden salad bowl

Homemade Dressing:

½ cup red wine vinegar

½ cup olive oil

2 tablespoons fresh herbs (parsley or dill), finely chopped

A splash pomegranate juice and seeds

Start by cutting the red stems off the swiss chard. Rinse and dry the leaves completely. These are added for a visual pop of color. I think they are too tough to eat raw. Place them inside the bowl as seen in the photo — just as a backdrop, but feel free to chop some and add to salad!

Preheat oven to 425 degrees. Peel 2 sweet potatoes (or yams). Dice into bite-sized cubes. Place on a baking sheet lined with parchment paper. Bake in the oven until tender about 20 minutes. Add a sprinkle of sea salt and some dried rosemary or any of the following dried herbs: basil, oregano, and parsley.

Next, rinse the radishes, dry and thinly cut. I soak them in the vinaigrette and then drain them. Or you may just salt these. I find radishes to be bland, so for this salad I wanted to impart some flavor.

Cut the pomegranate in half, place in a bowl of water. Break it apart and the seeds should sink to the bottom. Drain in colander and pick out any pulp.

Then be sure to choose 2 ripe avocados and cut into slices. Do this last-minute right before serving salad, as these tend to brown when exposed to air. Next, Rinse the arugula or baby kale and dry well.

Note: I always choose organic greens for all salads, as I tend to eat salad in bulk.

Cut the onions into very thin slivers and leave a few wider ones for a nice visual appeal — placing the larger ones on the top of salad.

Now assemble your salad:

Start by adding in the arugula or kale or a combo of them on top of the swiss chard inside the bowl. Then add in the thin slivers of red onion and mix with greens. Then add in diced roasted sweet potatoes. Next, add in a handful of dried cranberries and roasted pumpkin seeds, both dispersed evenly throughout the salad. Next, add in the radishes, I placed them in two clusters inside the bowl versus mixing with salad. Add the avocado slices along the side as seen in this photo. Sprinkle some pomegranate seeds all around for added color, texture and nutrients.

Toss with dressing right before serving. Everyone will want this recipe!

CHAPTER 5

Family Dinner Favorites

Italian Eggplant with Basil

Chicken and Rice Burrito Bowl

Marinated Flank Steak

Creamy Riced Cauliflower with Roasted Butternut Squash
and Crispy Mushrooms

Herbed Chicken Breast with Sundried Tomatoes, Kale and Rice

Smoked Gouda Butternut Squash Macaroni and Cheese

Charred Asian-Inspired Pulled Pork Tortillas with Carrot Slaw

Italian Eggplant
with Basil

. . . .

SERVES 4-6

When your garden is in full bloom, and bursting with yummy vegetables and herbs – this recipe is a great idea! It requires eggplant, basil, and you can add a few chunks of ripe tomatoes along with the sauce. This is farm-to-table cooking at its best! It is my all-time favorite meal that I could eat every single night. Pair this with my Armenian Sweet Bread (page 128) and a dollop of the Sour Cream Dip for an easy, healthy, and delicious dinner.

Ingredients:

3 medium eggplants, peeled and diced

½ large yellow onion, diced

1 (28 ounce) can San Marzano whole peeled tomatoes

1 cup jarred tomato sauce

1 bunch fresh basil

Sea salt and black pepper to taste

2 teaspoons Italian herbs, crushed

A good quality extra virgin olive oil

1 ½ cups water

Optional, 1 large tomato, cut into chunks

Non-stick large pan with lid

Garnish: fresh basil ribbons, dollop sour cream dip

. . . .

Sour Cream Dip:

1 cup light sour cream

Dried parsley flakes

Paprika

Sea salt

Dried Italian herbs

. . . .

Start by washing and drying the eggplant. Peel off the skin and dice into tiny bite-sized chunks. Set diced eggplant aside.

Next, dice the onion and heat a few good drizzles of olive oil in a pan. Sauté the onions for about 5 minutes until they become translucent. Add a dash of sea salt. Then add in diced eggplant. You will need to add in about 1 ½ cups of water. Let the eggplant simmer on low heat with a lid. It will release a lot of liquid. Salt it generously to flavor.

After the eggplant has simmered about 15-20 minutes, add in a can of San Marzano whole peeled tomatoes, and chop the tomatoes with a flat edge wooden spoon. Also, add in 1 cup of prepared jarred tomato sauce. Let this simmer about 10 minutes or until the eggplant is almost translucent and softens.

Measure 2 teaspoons of Italian dried herbs containing a combination of herbs: basil, oregano, rosemary etc. I like to crush them before I toss them into the dish. Also, add in about ½ cup of lightly packed fresh basil toward the end of the cooking process. Reserve some for the garnish.

Note: There is a recipe for making Homemade Italian Seasoning in Chapter 1 (page 17).

Continue cooking in pan until eggplant is very tender — another 20 minutes. I will serve it right from the pan for an easy summer meal. Be sure to taste it. It may need more herbs or salt!

I usually fill a bowl with eggplant and top with a dollop of Sour Cream Dip. Be sure to have my Armenian Sweet Bread on the side for dipping!

Hands down our favorite family meal! Enjoy.

Chicken and Rice Burrito Bowl

SERVES 6-8

Spice up tonight's dinner with my Chicken and Rice Burrito Bowl. This is my kid's favorite meal because it combines layers of delicious flavor in one big bowl. This is a meal I would serve when we have guests over. It includes cheesy rice, spicy shredded cooked-to-perfection chicken, sour cream, homemade guacamole, Black Bean & Corn Salsa, mashed black beans, shredded cheddar cheese along with the crispy flour tortillas for dipping — everybody's happy when this is served for dinner. If you are a vegetarian, skip the meat altogether, and pile on the mashed black beans, cheesy rice and toppings — equally good!

This delicious Mexican-inspired meal will put a little salsa in your step! Make the Black Bean and Corn Salsa and keep in fridge for 2 hours so flavors meld together before assembling this meal. Also, you will need to roast 2 chickens, so allow some time for that as well.

Ingredients:

2 roasted chickens

Black Bean and Corn Salsa (recipe follows)

1 large bag white flour tortillas

1 (29 ounce) can black beans, rinsed and mashed (for mashed black beans)

1 (28 ounce) can crushed tomato sauce

6-8 servings Basmati long grain rice, cooked

1 (16 ounce) can corn, charred

½ large yellow onion, diced

1 bunch of scallions, diced (use white and light green parts)

3 tablespoons tomato paste

½ large red onion, diced

5 fresh garlic cloves, diced

¼ teaspoon black pepper

½-1 teaspoon chili powder

1 packet of taco seasoning

1 teaspoon paprika

1 bunch fresh cilantro or parsley

A dash of garlic powder

Sea salt to taste

A good quality extra virgin olive oil

Topping recommendations: sour cream, guacamole, Black Bean and Corn Salsa (recipe follows), and hot sauce

Cheese Sauce:

2 tablespoons butter

2 tablespoons all-purpose flour

½ cup milk, warmed

1 bag shredded cheddar cheese

A dash of paprika

Sea salt and black pepper to taste

Black Bean and Corn Salsa:

1 (11 ounce) can black beans, rinsed

1 (11 ounce) can corn, rinsed

½ medium red onion, diced

2 tablespoons fresh cilantro, chopped

1 plum tomato, diced

1 tablespoon apple cider vinegar

½ lime freshly squeezed

A good quality extra virgin olive oil

Ground sea salt and black pepper to taste

Optional, diced red pepper, or hot peppers, seeded, and finely chop

In advance, prepare 2 whole cooked chickens. We are always pressed for time, so sometimes I use rotisserie chickens. If you have the time to cook the chickens - be sure to add some butter under the skin and salt it generously. Always check the internal temperature with a meat thermometer. Then let it rest and remove the skin and pull off all white and dark meat. I like to have extra chicken for some of my big eaters.

If you have more than you think you'll use, save some for chicken soup!

Dice the garlic cloves. Then dice a half of a yellow onion. In a large non-stick skillet heat a few drizzles olive oil and add diced garlic and onions. Add a few sprinkles of ground sea salt as well. Let this simmer on low heat until translucent, about 6 minutes.

Next, dice up the cooked chicken and add it to the skillet along with the garlic and onions. Add 1 can crushed tomatoes. Season with black pepper, paprika, chili powder, taco seasoning and a dash of garlic powder. Add the tomato paste, and half of the diced scallions (reserve some for later). Using a flat-edge spoon break up any chunks of chicken. Let this simmer on low heat for about 15 minutes just until flavors meld together. Then take off heat so it doesn't dry out.

In the meantime, while the chicken is simmering, prepare the mashed black beans. Drain the large can of black beans and rinse. Add them to a skillet along with a drizzle of olive oil and diced red onion. Mash the black beans with a flat edge spoon. Add in some chopped cilantro for added flavor and a pop of color. Cook for 4-5 minutes until warm. Add a dash of ground sea salt. Remove from heat. If it seems dry, add a little water.

Next, cook the Basmati long grain rice according to the directions on the box, or if you are pressed for time use the microwavable kind. In a small skillet toss in the remaining scallions along with a good drizzle olive oil. Open the corn and drain. Then add that to the skillet and let it heat up for a few minutes until it is slightly charred.

Once the rice is cooked, add it to a large bowl along with the scallions, charred corn and season with sea salt and black pepper. I also add a few drizzles of olive oil to make it moist. Alternatively, mix the rice with a Cheddar Cheese Sauce to make it rich and creamy.

MAKING THE CHEDDAR CHEESE SAUCE:

Start with a roux, add 2 tablespoons butter and in a saucepan and heat on low until melted. Then add 2 tablespoons flour, and whisk for 2-3 minutes until a paste develops.

Note: A roux (pronounced "roo") is equal parts butter and flour. It will serve to thicken your sauce and impart a slightly nutty flavor base. It is the cornerstone of French cuisine. Adding warmed milk (or liquid) won't stop the cooking process, so I highly recommend doing it this way. However, you may add in cold milk, but drizzle slowly and whisking constantly is important so the milk does not curdle — this way takes longer to cook.

Then whisk in ½ cup of warmed milk and a few handfuls shredded cheddar cheese. Season with paprika to develop that bright orange hue along with a sprinkle of black pepper and sea salt. If the sauce appears too thick, add in more warmed milk. If the sauce is still too loose, add in more cheese, and continue to heat until it thickens. Then mix with the rice.

MAKING THE BLACK BEAN AND CORN SALSA:

Open the can of black beans and corn, drain and rinse. Set these aside. Next, chop up half of a medium red onion. Cut the tomato in half and rinse out the seeds, then dice.

In a bowl, mix in the black beans, corn, chopped red onion, diced tomato, a drizzle of olive oil, 1 teaspoon apple cider vinegar, a squeeze half lime, sea salt, black pepper and chopped cilantro. Mix this well. Let it sit in the fridge for 2 hours to allow the flavors to meld together.

Taste the chicken and be sure it does not need further seasoning — an important step in the cooking process. You may garnish with chopped parsley or cilantro.

Assembling the burrito bowl:

You may serve this meal arranged on a large platter and let everyone create their own individual combinations.

Alternatively, you may serve it in one big tortilla bowl. I add multiple layers of tortillas overlapping in a pie shell and sprayed with a cooking spray. Then place a cake pan inside to flatten out the bottom. Then I baked it at 375 degrees (with a cake pan still inside) for about 12 minutes. Take the cake pan out and cook another 5 minutes until crispy and golden brown.

Next, load up your ingredients inside the bowl. For a pop of color and a finishing touch add some fresh chopped cilantro or parsley. Also, you may take the burrito bowl out of the pie shell and place on the platter for serving. It should hold together.

To serve with crispy tortillas — add a few drizzles of olive in a non-stick pan and add the flour tortillas one at a time to the pan. Heat about 3 minutes a side until crispy and golden brown. My daughter Maggie showed me how to cook these until super crispy. Adding a good amount of oil is the key!

Make a guacamole by mashing a few ripe avocados, a squeeze of lime, diced red onion, and a lot of ground sea salt. Cover so it doesn't brown.

Marinated Flank Steak

SERVES 4

Ingredients:

2 ½-3 lbs. flank steak, tenderize
to ¾-inch thickness

1 lime freshly squeezed

4-5 fresh garlic cloves, diced

½ cup parsley, chopped

½ cup of a good quality extra virgin olive oil

2 tablespoons apple cider vinegar

Ground sea salt

2 large plastic bags

Tenderizer

Grill pan or grill

Note: Keep this in mind when creating a good marinade, you'll need: salt, sugar, acid, oil and aromatics to increase the flavor profile of the meat. I have chosen to omit the sweetness in this marinade.

We love this marinade! This is a great meal for the athletes in the family. The steak requires 4-6 hours to marinate so plan accordingly!

Start by tenderizing the meat. This will break down the tough muscle fibers. Place inside a large plastic bag on a cutting board and pound out meat to about ¾-inch thickness. The more evenly you pound out the meat, the more evenly it will cook.

Next, heavily salt both sides with ground sea salt. Then place inside a new plastic bag. Add in a good drizzle — roughly ½ cup of olive oil, diced garlic, squeeze lime, chopped parsley and apple cider vinegar. Let this marinate in refrigerator for 4-6 hours or longer.

After 4-6 hours, take steak out of bag and pat dry. If the steak is wet, it won't sear properly. Let it rest at room temperature for 15-20 minutes. I use a non-stick grill pan to cook the steak if I am not grilling I outside. Add a drizzle of olive oil to the pan and heat on high heat. Place the steak in the pan and heat roughly 4-5 minutes a side. If you are grilling it, it will cook faster. Always check the internal temperature. Cook to desired temperature. We like ours medium rare about 135 degrees.

Turn off heat (or take off grill), and transfer to a wood cutting board with ridges on the side to catch the juices. Cover loosely and let steak rest for a 5-10 minutes to redistribute the juices. It is important to cut against the long grain otherwise the steak will be extremely chewy.

Use the juices from the steak as a sauce or deglaze the bits in the pan with some beef stock, add flour and stir until you have achieved the right consistency. Add in some mushroom and shallots. This is the kind of meal I would serve to Sydney the night before a big track meet!

In the summer when my cilantro is growing in abundance in my garden, we like this steak paired with chimichurri sauce, as seen in the photo at the beginning of this chapter.

Crispy Riced Cauliflower
with Roasted Butternut Squash and Cripsy Mushrooms

SERVES 6

My goal as a home chef is to feed my family with the healthiest ingredients possible which include lots of fresh vegetables. This Creamy Riced Cauliflower with Roasted Butternut Squash and Crispy Mushrooms along with the addition of smoked Gouda and a hint of crème fraîche is so delicious and nutritious. Say hello to your new favorite weekly meal.

Cremini mushrooms are also known as "baby bellas" or "baby portobello" mushrooms. These mushrooms are more intensely flavored than their more widely used cousin, the white button mushroom. Use a combination of mushrooms to create layers of flavor for this healthy meal.

Ingredients:

1 (20 ounce) package butternut squash, cubed and roasted

2 (12 ounce) packages fresh riced cauliflower

½ lb. sliced mushrooms, mixed variety: white button, baby bella, shitake

1 (32 ounce) container chicken stock (or vegetable stock) (use ¾ of container)

1 cup smoked Gouda, shredded

6 fresh sage leaves

½ sweet onion, diced

3-4 fresh garlic cloves, diced

A good quality extra virgin olive oil

2 tablespoons crème fraîche

A dash of turmeric and paprika

Black pepper and sea salt to taste

Red pepper flakes

Large non-stick skillet with lid

Start by preheating the to 425 degrees. Add the cubed squash to a baking sheet lined with parchment paper. Be sure to not overcrowd the pan, because you don't want them to steam, but to caramelize. Place in the oven roughly 20-25 minutes. If they are still firm, that is fine they will continue to cook in the broth.

Tip: I buy the butternut squash pre-cut. If you cannot find it this way, you can pre-cook it in microwave to soften it before you cut it. Be sure to prick it with a fork first. Then you can cut off the bottom about ½-inch, be sure it is stable on your cutting board and peel in downward motions. Then cut down starting at the neck, cutting in half lengthwise. Take out the seeds and cut with each half facing flat against your cutting board. It's essential to have a good, heavy chef's knife here!

In the meantime, add the diced onions and garlic to the pan with a drizzle of olive oil. Heat for 4-5 minutes or until translucent. Do not brown. Toss in 3-4 sage leaves and let these toast. The sage leaves will impart a nice flavor base into this dish. However, I take them out before serving as I find these too tough to eat.

In a separate cast iron skillet, add the sliced mushrooms and let these brown. This will take about 10 minutes. Be sure your mushrooms are dry when they go in the skillet, so they don't steam.

Once the onions and garlic are translucent, add both packages of riced cauliflower to the pan along with a few good drizzles of olive oil.

Be sure to have a lid that securely fits the pan. Let this steam until piping hot and translucent. Once cooked through, add in ¾ of the container of stock. I highly recommend using chicken stock for this recipe it creates a nice flavor for this dish, but if you are vegetarian feel free to swap it out for vegetable stock.

Next, add in the roasted butternut squash along with a few sprinkles of ground sea salt, black pepper, a dash of turmeric, and paprika to impart flavor and color. Last add a few good sprinkles of red pepper flakes for a spicy kick! Stir well to incorporate the seasonings.

Let this come to a boil, then reduce heat to a low simmer. You may add in the smoked gouda cheese. Be sure the pan is on low, so the cheese doesn't curdle. Mix continuously. Take off the heat once the cheese melts and swirl in crème fraîche. Taste it! You may need more pepper or salt.

Once the mushrooms have browned, add them to the top of the pan. Add a few fresh sage leaves as garnish only. Discard the mushy cooked ones.

In 30 minutes, you will have a warm, nourishing, and delicious meal for the family.

Herbed Chicken Breast
with Sundried Tomatoes, Kale and Rice

SERVES 4

This a great weeknight meal cooked and served in one pan. It checks all the boxes: carbohydrates, protein, fat, dairy, and vegetables. Easy clean up too!

Ingredients:

4 skinless chicken breast cutlets, roughly 2 lbs.

1 (8.5 ounce) jar julienne cut sundried tomatoes

1 (8 ounce) package burrata

1 (5 ounce) bag baby kale (or spinach), chopped

4-5 cups cooked brown and wild rice, unflavored

1 ½ teaspoons Italian herbs, crushed

1 (32 ounce) container chicken stock

1 small yellow onion, cut into slivers

1 bunch fresh basil, cut into ribbons

5 fresh thyme sprigs

3-4 fresh garlic cloves, thinly sliced

Ground sea salt

A good quality extra virgin olive oil

Balsamic vinegar or glaze

Optional, 2 tablespoons crème fraîche

Garnish, red pepper flakes

Ceramic coated cast iron skillet

Start by preheating the oven to 425 degrees.

First, prepare the chicken breasts. Generously salt both sides of breasts. Sprinkle both sides of breasts with Italian herbs. Drizzle tops of breasts with a balsamic vinegar. I use a vinegar that has the consistency of a balsamic glaze - its aged a long time and has a thick texture and tastes both tangy and sweet. Bake the chicken for 12 minutes, then flip. Cook another 12 minutes or more on the other side. Total cook time 25-35 minutes.

Always check internal temps of each breast with an instant read thermometer. Once done set these aside. You can even make these ahead of time and it will heat up in the pan with the broth.

Cover cooked chicken breast with foil and let it rest.

Next, cut half an onion into slivers. Then thinly slice garlic cloves. Add these to the skillet with a good drizzle of olive oil. Keep on medium low heat. Once translucent, about 5 minutes, add in half container of chicken broth (reserve the rest) along with a few sprigs of thyme for flavor — or remove the leaves from the stem so you don't have to fish the stems out later.

Cook the rice according to directions on box or use microwavable rice for easy clean up! Measure 4-5 cups of cooked rice and add to the skillet. Allow this to come to a boil and reduce heat. Let simmer for 10 minutes, covered.

Chop the baby kale, add to the skillet and stir well.

Use ¾ of the jar of sundried tomatoes and 1 tablespoon of the accompanying oil. Do not rinse tomatoes. Add julienne tomatoes and oil to the skillet. Save the rest for my Creamy Burrata with Sundried Tomatoes and Basil (page 52). Reduce heat to a low simmer.

Next, add in the chicken breast along with any juices that remain on the baking sheet. Add in a few more thyme sprigs.

Last, take off the heat, swirl in crème fraîche. Add the burrata as well. Garnish and flavor burrata with sea salt, olive oil, and red pepper flakes.

Cut a few handfuls of basil into ribbons and garnish dish and serve with garlicky Naan (page 131). Remove the thyme that cooked with the dish and add a few thyme sprigs to top of dish as garnish.

Cutting basil ribbons:

Stack 6-8 fresh basil leaves, one on top of the other and tightly roll. Then cut thin strips.

Smoked Gouda Butternut
Squash Macaroni and Cheese

SERVES 4-6

Macaroni and cheese gets a healthy makeover with this spicy creation that uses butternut squash as the base. The small amount of smoked Gouda adds a nice flavor, and the addition of sherry vinegar, red pepper flakes, paprika, pimentos, and black pepper kicks this up a notch. This is a home run — tastes great, budget friendly, and healthy, especially with the whole wheat pasta.

Ingredients:

¼ lb. smoked Gouda cheese, shredded

1 (20 ounce) package cubed butternut squash, roasted

A small handful freshly grated Pecorino Romano cheese

1 (lb.) box whole wheat penne pasta

1 small jar pimentos

A few dashes red pepper flakes

1 cup 2 % milk, warmed

2 tablespoons butter

2 tablespoons flour

½ tablespoon sherry vinegar

A dash of paprika, salt, black pepper

High-speed blender

Reserved pasta water

Start by preheating the oven to 425 degrees.

Place the pre-cut butternut squash onto a baking sheet lined with parchment paper. Drizzle with some olive oil. Place in the oven for about 35 minutes or until tender and caramelized. If you buy the butternut squash whole, pierce it, microwave to soften, cut in half lengthwise, take out seeds, and drizzle with olive oil and place face down to bake. Bake until tender, about 40 minutes

In the meantime, shred the smoked Gouda, and a small handful of Pecorino Romano cheese. Next, heat the milk for 30 seconds in the microwave or in small pot on the stove top.

Fill a large pot with water and heat on the stovetop. Once water boils, add pasta and make according to directions on the box. Reserve pasta water.

Using another pot, start the roux. Add butter, and once it melts whisk in the flour. These will be in equal proportions. Heat for 2-3 minutes until it forms a paste. Whisk in *warmed* milk and shredded cheeses. Keep heat on low.

Keep whisking until all the cheese has melted, and the cheese sauce is velvety smooth.

Once the squash is tender, add it to the blender along with a few tablespoons of pasta water — just enough water so you can easily blend it. Add in 3-4 pimentos slices, ½ table-spoon sherry vinegar and a few dashes of red pepper flakes. Blend for 2 minutes on high speed until everything is smooth.

Add the squash purée to the pot, along with a few dashes of paprika, to brighten the hue, and ground sea salt and black pepper to taste! Keep on low heat until the purée and cheese sauce have combined into a creamy sauce. Add in at least 1 ladle of pasta water, 2 if the sauce is too thick. Whisk until the cheese sauce is smooth and starts to thicken.

Using a spider strainer, add the cooked pasta to a large bowl. Then pour the butternut squash mixture over the pasta. Be sure that you do not need any more spice or sea salt. Adapt flavors according to your tastes. If it is still too thick, add more pasta water. Garnish as you wish.

Mix until all the pasta is coated with the butternut squash mixture and enjoy!

This photo was taken at the homeless shelter in the teaching kitchen. The women very artfully arranged everything!

Charred Asian-Inspired Pulled Pork Tortillas with Carrot Slaw

SERVES 8

Here is a list of components when making these delicious, mouth-watering tortillas. It will take roughly 5 hours to roast the pork, so plan accordingly.

Charred Asian-Inspired Pulled Pork Tortillas Ingredients:

1 (12 ounce) package soft white flour tortillas (6 –inches in diameter)

3 cups pulled pork (recipe follows)

Aioli Sauce (recipe follows)

Asian-Inspired Sauce (recipe follows)

Carrot Slaw (recipe follows)

1 small can corn, drained

1 bunch fresh cilantro

2 limes, 1 cut into wedges

1 orange, cut into wedges

Olive oil or sesame oil

Medium-sized non-stick pan

Tongs

Aioli Sauce:

A few tablespoons light mayonnaise

½ teaspoon Sriracha hot sauce

½ lime freshly squeezed

Asian-Inspired Sauce:

2 tablespoons hoisin sauce

2 tablespoons honey

3 tablespoons low sodium soy sauce

3 tablespoons rice vinegar

A drizzle olive oil or sesame oil

½ lime freshly squeezed

Carrot Slaw:

1 cup carrots, shredded

1 cup red cabbage, shredded

½ red onion, diced

2-3 tablespoons honey

A drizzle rice vinegar

½ lime freshly squeezed

Squeeze orange wedge

Ground sea salt

Pulled Pork:

5 ½-6 lb. pork shoulder roast — bone-in (also called Pork Butt)

1 (8 ounce) can cola

½ cup water

Ground sea salt

1 large onion cut into thick slices, pork will rest on this

Optional, garlic powder seasoning

Roasting pan with lid or aluminum foil, tightly cover

Start by making the pulled pork. Preheat the oven to 325 degrees.

PULLED PORK RECIPE:

The pork butt is located directly behind a pig's head and lies above the pig's shoulder blade, and although it is referred to as pork butt, it doesn't come from the back of the pig but the front. You can find pork shoulder/pork butt at the grocery store or butcher with bone in or boneless. This pork recipe comes out super tender and is neutral enough to be used in different cuisines.

This is a slow and low cooking process over a long period of time, roughly 5 hours. I know some chefs will go even lower and longer closer to 7 hours. This works great for my family though, and I am sure you will love the flavor! If you notice some excess fat on the roast just leave it until after it roasts, then cut it off. This will give the pork a great flavor. Allow the pork to sit out on the counter and come to room temperature for at least 30 minutes before cooking it.

Heavily salt pork with ground sea salt. You may season with garlic powder as well. Cut onion into thick quarters, and rest meat on onion slices, pour soda over pork, add in ½ cup water to pan. Tightly tent pork with aluminum foil and place on lowest rack in the oven for 4 hours. Halfway through, turn the pan.

After 4 hours, take off tenting and heat another 1 hour uncovered. If you feel the roast is browning too quickly, lower temperature to 300 degrees to finish roasting the last hour. The last hour to me is the most important as this is when the pork will start to brown — my favorite part.

At 5 hours, it should be well over safe internal cooking temperature, and the outside of the pork should be nicely brown.

Once done let pork rest for 5-10 minutes, then place on a cutting board. Pull using 2 forks. Reserve liquid.

While the pork is cooking that last hour, you can make the Asian-Inspired Sauce.

Combine hoisin sauce, honey, soy sauce, rice vinegar, a drizzle olive oil (or sesame oil) and a squeeze of half of a lime. Taste it to be sure you like the flavors. If the hoisin sauce is overpowering, add more soy sauce and lime.

MAKING THE CARROT SLAW:

Combine the shredded carrot, red cabbage slaw, chopped red onion, chopped cilantro, honey, rice vinegar, and finish it off with a squeeze of half of a lime and a squeeze of an orange wedge. Add sea salt as well. Most importantly, taste to be sure all the flavors are well balanced. Mix well!

Next, make the Aioli Sauce. Add a few tablespoons of light mayonnaise combined with ½ teaspoon Sriracha hot sauce (or more) and a squeeze of half of a lime. Taste! It should be very spicy, creamy and yummy! This adds a great kick to the tortillas.

Add the Asian-Inspired Sauce (reserve some) to a saucepan, along with 3 cups pulled pork (reserve the rest for other recipes) and combine. Heat on medium heat and let the flavors meld together. It may start to char a little from all the sugars, that makes it taste even better! I typically reserve a little sauce. You can add it to your tortillas in lieu of the aioli sauce if that's too spicy.

In the meantime, drain corn and set this aside. You may char the corn by adding it to a frying pan with a drizzle of olive oil — to add to the complexity of flavors. The key to great recipes is layering flavors!

Next, char tortillas (you can always do more). One of the guests at the homeless shelter taught me this trick. Light the stove top, keep on low heat and place 1 tortilla on the flame until charred, flip with tongs. Place them on a plate then cover until you have charred them all. Use extra care here. 30-45 seconds a side is about all you need.

NOW ASSEMBLE THE TORTILLAS:

Top a tortilla with pork, slaw, corn, Aioli Sauce, and cilantro for garnish. For a vegetarian option, just add more Carrot Slaw and, in this case, charred corn to add an extra layer of flavor. I eat it both ways ~ so good! Everyone will want to come for dinner!

With any remaining pulled pork, add reserved liquid and store in the fridge for up to 3 days.

Alternatively, if I am not making Charred Asian-Inspired Pulled Pork Tortillas, I pull the pork and place it back into the roasting pan with the juices. Then put it back into the oven for another 30 minutes to 1 hour at 200 degrees so the juices can impart more flavor. This will also keep it warm until I am ready to serve it.

Note: You may also cook pork shoulder in a crock pot — the key is you want it to fall apart!

SERVING SUGGESTIONS FOR PULLED PORK:
Mexican tacos

BBQ pulled pork sliders with cole slaw

Cuban and ham paninis, one of our favorites!

Pulled pork ragu

Cinque Terre, Italy

CHAPTER 6

Pasta, Pasta, Pasta!

Positano, Italy

Vallata, Italy, is where my father's family came from. It is in the region of Campania. My dad grew up calling pasta macaroni. He was the Italian chef in my family. He made the tomato sauce, meatballs and taught my mom (and eventually me) how to make the eggplant parmesan — there are fabulous old-world Italian recipes in my first cookbook — *Mariooch's Kitchen Food That Will Gather Your Family* for meatballs, pizza dough, eggplant parmesan, tomato sauce, Grandma's Italian bread, and Italian ricotta cheesecake, homemade ravioli and potato gnocchi as well as pasta making techniques.

When I was a little girl, I was enthralled by watching my Italian grandmother and Aunt Rose make ravioli from scratch. I was more of a spectator than an active participant, but nonetheless, I paid close attention to every fascinating detail — the mixing, the kneading, the stretching, the rolling, the cutting, the filling, and the precision — it was a masterpiece at work.

Watching the two of them cook was like listening to a symphony orchestra — their instruments were their hands — it was seamless and awe inspiring. My grandmother was a world class chef, but never followed a classic recipe — that made it hard to pass down recipes to the next generation. One reason, I created my first cookbook to record my families' recipes.

Grandma and Aunt Rose did things old-school like their mothers did in Italy. No machines or fancy gadgets were required. When you live in the foothills of a mountainous region far from stores — you work with what you have. You are not lugging a machine from house to house to make pasta. You put some muscle in it with a dash of patience, and viola (of course with practice) you have silky, smooth dough. Also, adding eggs to pasta was based on economics. If you could afford eggs and had easy access to them, you would toss a few in, but it wasn't necessary. The flour you used was based on the region you came from — as were the recipes. The combinations of flours to make pasta are endless — adding whole eggs, adding just the yolks, adding oils, the list goes on and on.

In this chapter, we will explore handmade pastas including cavatelli, ricotta cheese gnocchi, maltagliati using egg yolk dough, and some store-bought dried pasta mouth-watering creations. These are dishes that your family and friends will love.

Pasta History

It makes perfect sense that depending upon where you live in Italy, the dishes will be infused with what is in abundance in that region. For instance, the Campania region of Italy lies south of Rome along the Tyrrhenian Sea on the west coast of the Italian peninsula. Campania is a region celebrated for its climate, the fertility of the land, and the breathtaking landscapes.

This region includes well-known destinations such as Pompeii, the picturesque Amalfi coast, and the islands of Capri and Ischia. The Amalfi Coast is famous for the pastel-hued homes nestled in the enchanting towns of Positano, Amalfi, and Ravello deeply embedded in the cliffs and along the deep blue sea — a destination unlike no other in the world. It is truly a must-see if you go to Southern Italy. It is magical! I was lucky to have driven along the Amalfi Coast when I vacationed there with my parents — a memory I deeply cherish.

Campania is agriculturally rich in tomatoes, chestnuts, figs (my favorite), beans, peppers, onions, artichokes, potatoes, fennel oranges, lemons, and apples which all flourish in the rich volcanic soil under Mount Vesuvius. For those of you who are already thinking — San Marzano tomatoes come from there, you are correct! They grow in the rich soil at the foot of Mount Vesuvius. Some crops grow in great abundance like lemons, which are used to make limoncello, granita, and of course, pasta with lemons!

Those towns located along the coastline serve pasta tossed with freshly caught shellfish (and lemons) and fresh, still-warm mozzarella are just a few of the must-have dishes! Now, you are starting to get the idea of regional specific dishes.

Believe it or not, it was not until the 1840s that the first pasta recipe with tomatoes was documented. However, shortly thereafter, combining tomatoes with pasta dishes took hold, especially in the south of Italy — everyone fell in love with this combination including the rest of the world — especially Italian-Americans.

Pasta has evolved over time and is now considered more of a nutritionally complete dish with the addition of vegetables and meat, and one reason why I have dedicated an entire chapter to pasta. This chapter will teach you how to use the luxurious pasta water to create an emulsified sauce. It will teach you how to put a little muscle into your rolling pin when rolling out pasta by hand, it will teach you that handmade pasta is not difficult and debunk any misconceptions that have spread about how difficult it is! It will show you that making pasta can be a fun family activity that the kids will love.

Fresh Pasta Making

Pasta is a quintessential Italian cuisine with variations all over Italy. The truth remains that learning the techniques to make handmade pasta will be a lifelong gift to you and your family for generations to come. Handmade pasta is not that labor intensive, tastes so good, and is a budget friendly meal for the whole family. You can have a delicious meal in 30 minutes! The power to create delicious pasta is literally in your hands. Let's get to work!

Fresh Pasta Making Guide

- Making the dough — Mix in a stand mixer or by hand. If by hand, create a well with the eggs in the center and mix in the flour little by little on a wood board or in a bowl.

- Ideal texture should be pliable, not too sticky or too dry. If too dry, add a tablespoon of water at a time. If too wet, add a tablespoon of flour at a time.

- Knead for at least 5 minutes by hand.

- Cover & Rest dough.

- Divide & Conquer (work in small batches).

- Roll out the dough until slightly transparent and you can read print through it.

- For pasta machine attachment using the stand mixer, roll sections of dough into a narrow rectangle to fit machine and guide the dough with both hands.

- Once rolled, cut into shapes, noodles, bows, or make raviolis etc.

- Cook (use a large pot and generously salt water!)

- Use a spider strainer to fish out pasta.

Helpful Tips

- FLOUR — For a silky, supple dough buy double zero flour made in Italy– it's finely ground wheat flour -that has a powder-like consistency. All-purpose flour works great too — it's just more course, so you will need slightly more if you are substituting all-purpose flour for 00 zero in a recipe.

- SALT — optional in the dough, but ALWAYS add to boiling water

- Let the dough REST for 20-30 minutes.

- DIVIDE into 3-4 sections, working in small batches is easier.

- ROLLING — People have been rolling pasta by hand for centuries because it works! It takes lots of practice, but you will master it in time. A machine works great too and is good for a large volume.

- Using the stand mixer with a pasta machine attachment, roll out sections of dough into a narrow rectangle, dust each side with flour, and feed through machine. Be sure to guide the dough with both hands. On the first setting, feed the dough through, then fold it and feed it through again. As you get each narrower setting, feed through once or twice.

- ROLLING BY HAND — Work in small sections and keep flipping and rolling. I usually roll into a big rectangle. Be sure to flour the dough as you go.

- RULE OF THUMB is that you should be able to read print through the dough, then you know it is perfect!

- Buy a WOOD BOARD to roll and cut dough. Flour the work surface!

- Use a FRENCH ROLLING PIN — You'll have more control than a regular rolling pin. Keep flipping and turning it! (and flouring!)

- BOIL — Let pot of water come to a boil, add a generous amount of salt. Then add in pasta and cover to bring water back to a boil quickly. Once it boils, remove lid. You want the pasta to cook from the inside out. Raviolis are very delicate do not bring water to a rolling boil.

- SCOOP pasta out with a spider strainer or tongs.

- <u>SAUCE</u> — The pasta water is like liquid gold incorporate it into the sauce!

- <u>STORE</u> — Leave dough out for no more than 1 hour. Refrigerate for up to 4 hours or freeze. Use a food safe water bottle to spray dough if it feels dry. Cover unused dough.

"Cacio e pepe" means "cheese and pepper". It is one of our favorite sauces to pair with any pasta.

Making cacio e pepe is quite simple. First, make the pasta and reserve the pasta water. Add 2 tablespoons or more of butter to pan along with a good amount of cracked black pepper and toast. Add in reserved pasta water ¾ cup (or more). Mix to create a creamy sauce. Toss in pasta once done and wait until the liquids have emulsified and become a creamy and beautiful sauce. May add a drizzle of olive oil too.

Take off heat add lots of freshy grated cheese and more pepper! We really love freshly grated Pecorino Romano cheese, but Parmigiano Reggiano or Parmesan work great too.

Cooking is a creative process, taste as you go, experiment along the way, and have fun!!

Note: If using the stand mixer with pasta making attachment, always follow manufacturer's guidelines.

Handmade Cavatelli

SERVES 3-4

Cavatelli Dough Ingredients:

1 cup double zero flour

1 cup semolina flour (or semola finely ground "Rimacinata")

¼ cup water, drizzle a little at time

3 tablespoons of a good quality extra virgin olive oil

A sprinkle ground sea salt

2 tablespoons freshly grated Pecorino Romano cheese

8 ounces, whole milk ricotta cheese

Wood pastry board

Butter knife

Non-stick frying pan

Large, wide pot

Stand mixer

MAKING THE HANDMADE CAVATELLI:

Measure 1 cup ricotta cheese. If there is a lot of moisture, you can strain it. Add the cheese to a stand mixer along with 3 tablespoons olive oil and mix 2 minutes until smooth and creamy. Add to that a sprinkle of ground sea salt and 2 tablespoons Pecorino Romano cheese, mix for 2 minutes.

Next, measure 1 cup each of double zero and semolina flours. Be sure to spoon and level the flours. Precision is important here. Turn the mixer off and add the flours and mix until you have achieved the desired consistency. Alternatively, you can mix in a bowl using your hands to combine ingredients.

Dough should be pliable and not sticky or dry. If dry, add more oil or water, if too wet add 1 tablespoon at a time of flour.

Knead the dough on the wood board for 5 minutes and shape into a ball. Let dough rest covered for 30 minutes. Cut off a chunk and roll into a long rope.

Work on a wood board lightly dusted with semolina flour. Roll the rope thin, but not so thin that it breaks. Cut off 1-inch pieces in length. Then using the butter knife, place the knife in the center of the piece and drag it along the board toward you using the ridges in the knife creating a separation on the inside.

As you make a pile start to add them to a baking sheet lined with parchment paper and sprinkled with semolina flour. These can stay uncovered for up to 1 hour. After that, refrigerate for up to 4 hours, otherwise freeze on a baking sheet until solid, then toss in a freezer bag.

Cook the cavatelli in salted boiling water for 8 minutes.

Garlic and Sage Infused
Butter Cream Sauce

. . . .

Ingredients:

3 tablespoons butter

2 fresh garlic cloves, whole

A few fresh sage leaves

1 heaping tablespoon crème fraîche

Pecorino Romano cheese, freshly grated

Fresh chives or fresh basil ribbons "chiffonade"

Cracked black pepper

. . . .

MAKING THE GARLIC AND SAGE INFUSED BUTTER CREAM SAUCE TO PAIR WITH HANDMADE CAVATELLI:
Add butter to skillet along with a drizzle of olive oil, whole garlic cloves, and a few sage leaves to infuse some flavor and aromatics into the sauce...toss in half the cavatelli and add in a ladle or 2 of pasta water. After 3 minutes, take off heat, add in a heaping tablespoon of crème fraîche — stir well.

I like working in small batches using a smaller pan. Cook only half the cavatelli at a time. While you toss the cavatelli with the cream sauce, start boiling the next batch using the same pasta water. Pour the cavatelli with cream sauce in a bowl. Discard the sage leaves and garlic.

Then clean pan and start the sauce again so you can toss it with the next batch of cavatelli. Toss the pasta with sauce and serve.

Plate the pasta with a good shaving of Pecorino Romano cheese, cracked black pepper, and fresh chopped chives or fresh basil ribbons. Enjoy!

Chiffonade is the process of slicing fresh basil leaves or other delicate herbs into thin ribbons. Stack the leaves on top of each other, gently roll them, and then use a sharp knife to slice into thin ribbons.

Maltagliati Pasta
(Egg Yolk Dough)

SERVES 3

These pasta pieces shaped into squares, triangles or rhombuses started as the remains of rolled out tagliatelle pasta dough or re-kneaded ravioli cuttings. They have evolved over time into their own delicious pasta!

Egg Yolk Dough — this beautiful yellow hued dough recipe has a richness and firmness to it because the addition of egg yolks. You can use this dough to make other types of pasta too. I like pairing it with a savory sauce like the Garlic and Sage Infused Butter Cream Sauce.

Cut into 3-inch shapes: squares, triangles or rhombuses. Cook 2-3 minutes and sauce. This pasta lends itself to imperfections which are akin to life — nothing is perfect! It's a delicious reminder.

Egg Yolk Dough Recipe:

1 ½ cups double zero flour
(or 1 ¾ cups all-purpose flour)

9 yolks (use large eggs)

1 tablespoon of a good quality extra virgin olive oil

4-5 tablespoons water

Wood board

Rolling pin

Stand mixer with pasta attachment
(or make by hand)

Large, wide pot

The Steps to Making Egg Yolk Dough:

Step 1:

You will need 2 bowls. Crack open the eggs, separate the yolks from the whites. It is fine if a little of the egg whites get mixed in with the yolks. Mix the yolks with a fork. (Save the egg whites for scrambled eggs!)

Step 2:

Add the flour, egg yolks, and 1 tablespoon olive oil to the stand mixer along with 4 tablespoons water. Mix until you have achieved the desired consistency. Dough should be pliable, not tacky. If tacky add more flour 1 tablespoon at a time.

Step 3:

Place dough onto a lightly floured work surface and knead the dough with the palms of your hands for 5-10 minutes.

Step 4:

Cover and rest the dough 20-30 minutes.

Step 5:

Divide the dough into 3-4 sections. Roll with the rolling pin into a narrow rectangle to fit through the pasta machine, be sure to dust, or roll out into a large rectangle if rolling by hand. Add flour to both sides so it doesn't stick. Refer to my Fresh Pasta Making Guide in this chapter (page 107).

Step 6:

If using a machine, feed through machine on lowest setting, fold, feed through again. Then increase setting and feed through, repeating the process until you have achieved a thin dough sheet and can read print through it. Feed through each setting once or twice, dusting both sides. If doing by hand, roll out into a large rectangle until you can read print through it.

Step 7:

Making the Maltagliati Pasta.
Cut the pasta into 3-inch shapes: squares, triangles or rhombuses.

Step 8:

Place on a baking sheet lightly dusted with flour. Cover until you are ready to cook it. If dry give it a spritz of water.

Step 9:

Bring a large pot of water to a boil and add a generous amount of salt. I use table salt. Add pasta and give it a quick stir. Cover to bring back to a boil, then uncover. Cook for 2-3 minutes. Cook pasta in 2 batches.

Step 10:

Next, prepare your sauce and toss pasta. Enjoy!

Pasta Primavera
with Creamy Artichoke Sauce

SERVES 4-6

My husband loves to order pasta primavera when we eat out, so I wanted to recreate this dish for dining in. This is a rich and creamy dish without the addition of heavy cream. It is made with a combination of puréed artichokes along with a hint of crème fraîche and Pecorino Romano cheese as well as slices of mushrooms and broccoli. Artichoke dip meets pasta in this fabulous and delicious, creamy dish! Add some burrata for an even creamier texture that will send this dish over the top.

Ingredients:

1 (1lb.) box tricolor fusilli pasta

½ cup Pecorino Romano cheese, freshly grated

1 ½ cups broccoli florets

1 small box button mushrooms, sliced

1 (12 ounce) jar chopped or whole artichokes (in oil)

1 ½ cups chicken stock

2 heaping tablespoons crème fraîche

¼ cup Vidalia onion, finely diced

½ large red onion, cut into slivers

1 bunch fresh basil, cut into ribbons

A good quality extra virgin olive oil

1 ladle of pasta water (or more)

Ground sea salt to taste

Optional, add burrata to make it extra creamy

High-speed blender

Large non-stick pan

Fill a large pot with water and add in broccoli florets, let it cook until its bright green. Then drain and run under cold water to retain that bright color. This cooking process is called blanching in which a food, usually a vegetable, is placed in boiling water briefly, and finally plunged into cold water to halt the cooking process.

Now add water to the large pot and bring to a boil. Add the pasta and cook according to the directions on the box. Add a generous amount of salt.

Next, add a few good drizzles of olive oil to a medium-sized cast iron skillet. Finely dice the Vidalia onion and sauté for 2 minutes until translucent. Then add in the jar of chopped artichoke hearts. Let these cook for 5 minutes. Add some ground sea salt.

Transfer the onions and artichokes to a high-speed blender and blend them along with 1 cup of chicken stock (reserve ½ cup) — do a little at a time until you achieve a smooth and creamy consistency.

Then add the mixture back into the pan. Slice the mushrooms and add them to the cream sauce along with the red onion slices (save some for garnish) as well as ½ cup more of chicken stock. Simmer on low for 5 minutes.

Using a spider strainer fish out the pasta and add to pan. Reserve some pasta water. Mix to incorporate all the flavors. Add a few sprinkles of ground sea salt. Next, add in 2 heaping tablespoons of crème fraîche. Mix well. Then add in the cooked broccoli florets. Top with the Pecorino Romano cheese. Take off heat and mix well.

For garnish top with basil ribbons, and red onions slices. Keep some pasta water so you can add more to keep the sauce creamy. As it cools, the sauce will thicken. You may add some burrata balls and cut into them to make this pasta dish even more creamy and delish! Serve with a rustic, crusty Italian bread.

Alternatively, if you prefer less pasta you may use only half of the box and add more broccoli.

Healthy Penne Alfredo

SERVES 4

This is a rich, creamy, savory and satisfying meal that my family adores! White beans and cooked cauliflower are puréed to create this creamy sauce and cut down on the butter and omit the cream altogether. They have a neutral taste, so you cannot detect them whatsoever! Butter, cream, and Parmesan cheese are classic ingredients in alfredo sauce. This is one of those creative and healthy spins on a classic alfredo. It will thicken up as it sits, so reserve the pasta water to add if you need it!

Ingredients:

1 (lb.) box penne or fettucine (¾ box)

1 cup frozen riced cauliflower (or fresh riced cauliflower)

1 (15.5 ounce) can northern white beans, rinsed (use ¾ can)

½ medium yellow onion, diced

½ shallot, diced

1 bulb fresh garlic, roasted

½ teaspoon crushed garlic, jarred

1 cup milk

2-3 tablespoons herbed or regular salted butter

8 baby bella mushrooms, thinly sliced

¾ cup Parmesan, freshly grated (more for shaving)

A good quality extra virgin olive oil

Red pepper flakes, sea salt and black pepper

High-speed blender

Ceramic coated cast iron skillet

Start this recipe by roasting the garlic.

ROASTING THE GARLIC:

Preheat oven to 400 degrees. Cut top off 1 garlic bulb, exposing the cloves, and drizzle with olive and place on a baking sheet. Place in oven for 20-25 minutes. Roasted garlic is great for making hummus, dips, cream sauces. The roasting process takes away the bitter garlicy flavor — it is especially good in this dish! Once the garlic is ready, proceed to the next step.

Cook ¾ of the box of pasta according to directions on the box. Allow roughly 10-12 minutes to cook pasta. You can use the whole box, but I find that the pasta absorbs too much of the sauce and the starch thickens it, so try ¾ box and the outcome will be creamier. Be sure to generously salt the pasta water. Reserve pasta water

Next, heat the frozen riced cauliflower according to directions on the bag. Then, rinse and drain ¾ of the can of white beans. Set these aside.

Then add 3 tablespoons butter, herbed butter is even better if you have it, a drizzle olive oil and the diced onions to the pan. Heat until translucent. Now, add 1 cup of cooked riced cauliflower to pan with onions. Cook 1 minute to meld flavors together. If you are using a fresh riced cauliflower, add to pan with onions and be sure to cover the pan with a tight-fitting lid. The fresh riced cauliflower will take roughly 8 minutes. Let simmer until translucent.

Transfer cauliflower, onions, and white beans to blender. Season the mixture with sea salt and red pepper flakes. Add a tiny drizzle of water and 6 cloves roasted garlic to the blender, hold the remaining cloves for another recipe. Simply squeeze the clove from the roasted garlic. Purée until creamy and liquified, adding more water as needed.

Next, add the cauliflower-white bean purée to pan, keep heat on low. Heat 1 cup milk in a small pot or microwave. Then add the warmed milk to the pan and add in about ¾ cup finely shredded Parmesan cheese. Stir continuously. Season well with black pepper, ground sea salt, and more red chili flakes. Taste the mixture. You can season further If you wish.

In the meantime, rinse and pat dry the mushrooms. Thinly slice. These add a nice flavor to this dish! Add the sliced mushroom to the pan.

Scoop pasta with a spider strainer add to pan and mix. If the sauce thickens add some pasta water to loosen it. Taste it to be sure it is to your liking. Take off the heat and add a generous shaving of Parmesan to the top. Serve right from the pan. You will love this so much!

Sweet Potato Cheese Sauce
with Pappardelle Pasta

SERVES 4-6

Super easy and healthy weeknight meal that everyone will love. This sauce tends to thicken, so keep extra pasta water on hand to loosen it.

Ingredients:

3 cups sweet potato or yam

¾ cup Parmesan cheese, freshly grated (more for shaving)

1 tablespoon crème fraîche

2 tablespoons sweet onion, diced

1 tablespoon salted & roasted pumpkin seeds

1 bunch fresh chives, chopped

1 pomegranate

Sea salt & ground pepper

1 cup pasta water

1 lb. box of pappardelle

Paprika

Red pepper flakes

Garnish: pomegranate seeds and pumpkin seeds

Large non-stick frying pan

High-speed blender

Cook potatoes in the microwave, let cool completely before handling them. Scoop out the inside and measure 3 cups of sweet potatoes. I find the organic sweet potatoes/yams tastes sweeter, so I tend to buy them. They are interchangeable in stores, so just look for the deep orange colored potatoes for this recipe.

Note: You may bake the potatoes in the oven as well. Just be sure to do that in advance. It can take up to 1 hour (or more) to bake.

In the meantime, make the pasta according to the directions on the box. Add a generous amount of salt once pasta comes to a rolling boil.

Using a large size frying pan, drizzle in some olive oil and add in the onions. Sauté until translucent. Next, add 3 cups cooked sweet potatoes and onions to the blender along ½ cup of pasta water, and pumpkin seeds. Blend for 1 minutes until completely puréed.

Then add sweet potato purée to the frying pan along with crème fraîche, Parmesan cheese, sea salt, black pepper and a few sprinkles of paprika. Mix well and take off the heat.

Next, add the pasta to the pan and stir. Add in the remaining ½ cup of pasta water (or more). Do not discard the pasta water. Chop up the chives and add to the pan as a garnish.

Remove the seeds from pomegranate and add in a small handful to pasta. Garnish with more chives on top and a tiny sprinkle Parmesan cheese to garnish. To give this a spicy kick add some red pepper flakes! You can even blend some red pepper flakes into the sauce as well. Dinner is served!

Sage Butter Ricotta Gnocchi

. . . .

SERVES 3-4

Ingredients:

1 (15 ounce) container whole milk ricotta cheese

1 cup double zero flour or all-purpose flour

2 large egg yolks

⅓ cup Pecorino Romano cheese,
freshly grated (more for shaving)

3 tablespoons butter

Ground sea salt

Cracked black pepper

A pinch of nutmeg

A few fresh sage leaves

Table salt

Cast iron skillet or frying pan

Gnocchi board or fork

Extra flour for dusting

Stand mixer

Large, wide pot

. . . .

You may strain the ricotta cheese if it has a lot of moisture. Place it inside the stand mixer and add in the 2 yolks and mix on low for 2 minutes until smooth and creamy.

Next, add in about ⅓ cup Pecorino Romano cheese along with a few sprinkles ground sea salt and cracked black pepper as well as a *tiny* pinch of nutmeg. Mix these ingredients for 2-3 minutes until completely smooth.

Measure 1 cup of flour (I prefer double zero for this recipe) and add it to the stand mixer. Mix on low until the dough forms together. Turn the mixer off and feel the dough. It should be pliable, soft and easy to work with. If you feel it's a bit wet, add a tablespoon at a time of flour and mix until you have achieved a soft dough.

Note: if you use all-purpose flour add ¼ cup more to this recipe.

Turn the dough onto a clean floured work surface. Shape dough into a ball and flatten into a disc about 7 inches wide. Let dough rest covered 30 minutes.

Then cut 6 slices using a pastry scrapper. Roll each piece out into a rope or dowel about ¾-inch thick. Cut tiny squares about ¾-inches. This should make about 3-4 servings, but honestly my son can eat this whole batch, so plan your servings accordingly!

Fun facts: Depending upon where you come from in Italy everyone has different techniques for making gnocchi. Have fun experimenting.

After cutting the gnocchi, use different techniques to shape the gnocchi:

1. Leave them in tiny pillow-like squares

2. Roll them on a gnocchi board to create the ridges.

3. Using the gnocchi board and pull them with your thumb to make a slight separation comparable to the cavatelli.

4. Press one side of each piece against the tines of a fork (dipped in flour) to make indentations.

The classic ridges help the sauce cling to the surface of the gnocchi. Some feel that you don't want to overwork the gnocchi dough and therefore leaving the gnocchi in the pillow-like square is best for a lighter gnocchi texture.

MAKING THE SAGE BUTTER SAUCE:

Heat 3 tablespoons butter in the cast iron skillet, add in about 6 sage leaves. Keep heat on medium low. You want to toast the sage leaves until crispy. The butter should bubble a little, but do not let it brown. If you do let the butter brown, then this recipe is called Browned Butter Sage Ricotta Gnocchi, and I am sure it will still be exceptionally good!

Fill a large pot with water and let it come to a boil. Add a good amount of table salt and drop in half the gnocchi. Be sure to place the lid back on so the pot comes back to a boil. Once it boils, remove the lid. Cook for 2 minutes, until they float to the top.

Drain gnocchi using a spider strainer and add to the frying pan or cast iron skillet. Toast gnocchi for 2 minutes. Then take out of the pan and add to a bowl. Add more butter to the pan and heat on low.

In the meantime, cook the remaining gnocchi. Drain well and add to the skillet. Reserve a little pasta water. Cook for 2 minutes or more until lightly browned.

Add all the gnocchi back into the skillet. Add a good amount of cracked black pepper, a tiny sprinkle of sea salt and mix.

Take off the heat, add Pecorino Romano cheese, and a tablespoon (or more) of reserved pasta water and mix well until all the cheese melts. Taste it and be sure it is well seasoned. Serve immediately!

Use gnocchi in soups. Cook gnocchi and then add a red sauce in lieu of the Sage Butter Sauce. Another one of my favorites is to pair the gnocchi with a mushroom cream sauce.

Use gnocchi for macaroni and cheese and bake in the oven with breadcrumbs on top.

There are many possibilities with gnocchi. It's a family favorite and the reason I wanted to add it to my cookbook.

If you wish to freeze, you may place on a baking sheet lined with parchment paper and dusted with flour, allow them to freeze then transfer to a bag and place in the freezer. Add an extra minute or more to cooking time. Test one, and taste it, then adjust the time accordingly.

For a quick red sauce use San Marzano tomatoes, break them apart using a flat edge spoon, add salt, black pepper, and a drizzle of olive oil and some red chili flakes. Toss the gnocchi with this easy and quick homemade sauce.

CHAPTER 7

Homemade Breads, Bagels and Pretzels

I have fond memories of watching my Italian grandmother braid loaves of bread for the holidays. At Eastertime she would shape the bread into a wreath and add colorful hard-boiled eggs. Making homemade bread was a family specialty and one I have perfected with the breads in this chapter. Grandma's home-made Italian bread is in my first cookbook — that is another great recipe that took me much time to learn and perfect.

My Armenian Sweet Bread (pictured in this photo) is a recipe my family loves so much. It can be made into a wreath as well.

I make these breads all-year round and they are loved by everyone including family, friends and neighbors. I chose to include a Naan rec-ipe as it's so easy to whip up any night of the week. The Pepperoni Pinwheels are a great appetizer or lunch, and the Savory Zucchini Bread is one of my favorites. My Easy NY Style Bagels are great for the weekends. The Cinnamon-Sugar Pretzels are great any day of the week.

Bread is the symbol of nourishment — I can think of no greater joy than to feed my family and nourish them.

Armenian Sweet Bread

YIELDS 2-3 LOAVES

My husband loves this bread so much that when I first started making it, he wanted me to open a bakery just to sell the bread ~ true story! This Armenian Sweet Bread or Easter Bread, also called choereg or sometimes choreg, is a buttery sweet bread, fragrant with spices, called mahleb, along with nigella seeds. It is a delicious bread that will be devoured in minutes and is wonderful to make any time of year. Best of all, this bread can be made in advance and keeps beautifully frozen.

Sweet bread is popular in many cultures around the world, with many variations. This original recipe is Armenian which includes the ground mahleb and ground nigella seeds as well as the sesame seeds added at the end to the top of the bread. It tastes like the ever-popular challah bread but is denser.

Ingredients:

6 cups all-purpose flour

1 ½ sticks salted butter, softened

1 cup whole milk (or 2% milk)

½ cup granulated sugar

3 large eggs

1 ½ teaspoons table salt

1 packet active dry yeast (dissolve in ½ cup warm water)

3 egg yolks, for egg wash

A good quality extra virgin olive oil

Optional, 1 teaspoon mahleb, ground

Optional, 1 teaspoon nigella, ground

Optional, sesame seeds and poppy seeds

Hand mixer

First, set your oven temperature to 350 degrees. Then dissolve 1 packet of yeast in ½ cup of warm water and give it a stir. It should look like murky water. Let it rest a minute. If the granules do not dissolve, check the expiration date on the yeast — it may be expired.

Next, warm milk in a microwave save bowl 30 seconds. Place butter in the microwave for 30 seconds as well. You can also leave it out at room temperature to let it soften.

In a large bowl, mix in the yeast, stir in the sugar, salt, milk, and the softened (not melted) butter. Mix 3 whole eggs separately then toss them in as well. You may add in the ground nigella and mahleb seeds at this time or you may omit this step. Mix well. Then add flour 1 cup at a time.

Note: You may use a hand mixer for the wet ingredients. Once I mix the wet ingredients and dry ingredients together, I use a spoon to mix everything. It's easier this way. It's a lot of dough, so mixing by hand is best.

This dough will be very sticky. Knead the dough on a clean and lightly floured work surface. I use a pastry mat. After about 10 minutes of kneading, toss it back into the bowl and lightly grease the bottom of the bowl with olive oil and then add a drizzle to the top of the ball of dough, cover and put in a warm place to rise. After roughly 1 ½ hours I will check it, and it usually has doubled in size.

> *If I want my dough to rise for any bread recipe, I turn my oven on to 350 degrees for 30 minutes. Place the dough inside a metal bowl, tightly covered, and on the stovetop until it doubles in size. This works well.*

Once the dough has doubled in size, cut the loaf into 3 sections if you are making 3 loaves or 2 sections if baking 2 loaves. Working with 1 section at a time, divide it into 3 pieces. Then roll out each piece into a long rope. Combine the 3 ropes together at one end and tuck it under, then braid the pieces like you would a braid, and seal the other end and tuck that under as well. Practice makes perfect!

Place each braided load onto a baking sheet lined with parchment paper. Then cover each loaf until it puffs up, roughly 30 minutes. I will place these on my stovetop and turn my oven on to 350 degrees. The heat from the oven helps the bread to expand. Once the loaf has puffed up, brush on the egg yolk wash, and add the sesame seeds and poppy seeds. You can do just sesame, just poppy, or a combination of the two, or no seeds at all!

MAKING THE EGG WASH:

Separate the white of the egg from the yolk. Mix the 3 yolks with a fork and evenly spread onto the bread using a pastry brush. Be generous. You may skip this step if you are skipping eggs. It will still taste great!

Then place in the oven at 350 degrees for roughly 20-24 minutes. The bread will be a rich, deep golden, brown color when it is down. Let it cool on a cooling rack for 5 minutes. Also, you may bake 3 loaves at a time if you have a convection fan in your oven to circulate the air around. I have done that but move the bread onto different racks at least once, so they bake evenly. I do prefer baking 1 loaf at a time, albeit tedious.

This bread has become a family favorite, not just at Eastertime, but anytime of the year.

Naan

. . . .

YIELDS 8

Naan is a family and friend favorite. My friend says it reminds her of traditional Tandoor — however my version is cooked on the stovetop in a piping hot cast iron skillet. It is bubbly, airy, puffy and oh so good! In a separate pan you can melt butter, add chopped garlic and herbs then spread it on the naan. Sometimes I will make it and then create a sandwich — in this case we call them Naanwiches!

Dough Ingredients:

4 cups all-purpose flour

¼ cup warm water

1 tablespoon granulated sugar

1 package active dry yeast

¾ cup whole or 2% milk, warmed

¾ cup plain Greek yogurt

½ teaspoon table salt

. . . .

Other Ingredients:

1 stick salted butter

4 fresh garlic cloves, finely diced

Chopped fresh herbs (parsley or chives)

A good quality extra virgin olive oil

Cast iron skillet with lid

Non-stick pan

Rolling pin

Stand mixer with hook attachment

. . . .

Start by measuring ¼ cup warm water and add 1 packet of yeast and give a quick stir. Add to the bowl of the stand mixer along with sugar and let sit for 5 minutes. It should be foamy. Next, add in warmed milk, yogurt, salt and mix.

Add in flour 1 cup at a time. Once the dough forms together, turn it out onto a lightly floured surface and knead the ball of dough for 5 minutes. Then place it in a bowl and cover for 30 minutes in a warm spot.

Flatten dough and cut into 8 equal sized pieces. Roll each piece into a ball. Roll each ball out — one at a time using a rolling pin. Roll it out about ½ inch thick and 6-8 inches in diameter, depending upon the size of the skillet. Cover the unused dough.

Melt half the butter and coat the dough on both sides using a pastry brush. Place in the hot cast iron skillet — be sure to add olive to pan so it doesn't stick — a little drizzle before each naan goes into skillet.

Heat covered for 1 minute or so until those big bubbles form, then flip and take lid off, another 2 minutes.

Note: Use extra caution and place skillet on a back burner. Gently place the dough in the skillet so there is no splatter of hot oil. When you put the lid on you should see the steam circulating throughout the pan. Turn vent on high to remove any smoke and use oven mitts when handling the skillet.

Remove the cooked naan with a pair of tongs. Place on plate and cover with two clean dish towels. Repeat with remaining dough.

For dipping: In a non-stick pan add olive oil and chopped garlic. Heat for 2-3 minutes, add ½ stick butter and allow that to melt. Then add in ½ cup chopped fresh parsley or chives just to warm. Take off heat.

Pair with my Spicy Moroccan Chickpea Soup (page 69), any of my salads or you can even eat for breakfast with some my Herbed Cream Cheese (page 28) and fruit.

Pepperoni Pinwheels

YIELDS 18

My Pepperoni Pinwheels are a spin off from Valya which is an Albanian bread my husband ate growing up. My kids love these pinwheels for lunch on the weekends. I make them extra spicy with lots of black pepper, paprika and oregano, but you can tone down the spice as well. With that said, you can also spice it up with red pepper flakes. Skip the pepperoni if you don't eat meat. Either way you choose to make these they are delicious!

Dough Ingredients:

3 cups all-purpose flour, excess flour for dusting

1 stick salted butter, melted

1 teaspoon salt

½ cup water

1 packet active dry yeast, dissolved in ¼ cup water

Wood board

Rolling pin

Stand mixer with hook attachment

Pepperoni Pinwheels:

2 cups shredded mozzarella cheese

1 (7 ounce) package pepperoni

Ground sea salt

Paprika

Oregano

Black pepper

Red pepper flakes

A good quality extra virgin olive oil

1 cup jarred tomato sauce for dipping

Preheat oven to 350 degrees.

Add 1 packet active dry yeast to the stand mixer, add in ¼ cup warm water and give it a stir. Add to the bowl of a stand mixer and let it sit for 5 minutes. After 5 minutes, add in the melted butter, salt, an additional ½ cup water, and the 3 level cups all-purpose flour. Mix for 1-2 minutes until it forms into a dough. Should come together easily.

Next, roll dough onto a floured wood board and knead for 5 minutes. Add a few drizzles of olive oil into the bowl of the stand mixer. Place ball of dough back in the metal bowl and add a drizzle of oil on top. Cover tightly. Place on the stovetop so the heat from the oven encourages dough to rise. After 30 minutes, turn off the oven.

Let dough rise for about 1 hour. It should double in size. Divide dough in half and on a lightly floured surface, roll out into a very thin rectangle.

Drizzle oil onto the dough and with your hands spread it onto the dough and add a good sprinkling of sea salt. Next, add paprika with a heavy hand onto the entire surface area of the dough, no white spots remaining. Next, add oregano and black pepper to your tastes. Red chili flakes add a nice touch!

Measure roughly 1 cup of shredded mozzarella and add to the rectangle dispersing it all over the surface. Last is to add pepperoni on top of the mozzarella. Add as much pepperoni as you like, but not so much you can't roll it. I usually use the entire package by the time I am done making both rolls.

Tightly roll, cut into pinwheels. Arrange on a baking sheet lined with parchment paper and press them down a little. Bake for 20 minutes at 350 degrees and raise temperature to 400 degrees for the last 3 minutes. Bake until golden on the bottoms. Repeat the process, using the other half of dough.

They will puff when you bake them. Serve with a side of warmed jarred tomato sauce for dipping!

Savory Zucchini Bread

SERVES 8

This recipe is savory with just the right hint of sweet. The combination is delicious, springy and moist. Serve this bread with a spicy soup or enjoy with a hot cup of coffee for breakfast. Either way, this bread is decadent and will vanish quickly so make 2. I prefer using a cake pan as I find it cooks more evenly than in a loaf pan. This is nothing like you have ever tasted before and it takes zucchini bread to a whole new level! You will love it.

Ingredients:

2 ½ cups grated zucchini with skin (2 medium zucchinis)

1 (8.25 ounce) can creamed corn

2 cups all-purpose flour

1 large egg

¾ cup light sour cream

1 cup fresh cilantro, chopped

¾ cup vegetable oil

1 cup granulated sugar

1 teaspoon baking powder

1 teaspoon baking soda

½ teaspoon ground ginger

½-¾ teaspoon black pepper

1 tablespoon taco seasoning packet, mild (or Mexican seasoning)

⅓ cup Mexican or spicy cheese, finely shredded

10-inch cake pan

Stand mixer with paddle attachment

Start by preheating the oven to 350 degrees.

Grate the zucchini and measure 2 ½ cups. Be sure to save some for garnish. Pack each cup so you get as much in as possible. Add this to the bowl of the stand mixer.

Then add to that, the beaten egg, Mexican cheese, taco seasoning, sour cream, creamed corn, vegetable oil, ground ginger, black pepper, chopped cilantro, and sugar. The sugar will serve to make the outside of this bread a golden brown and add just the right hint of sweet. Mix these ingredients well until they are fully combined.

Next, in separate bowl, whisk together the dry ingredients: white flour, baking powder, and baking soda. Be sure these are fully incorporated. Then combine the wet ingredients and the dry ingredients and mix until smooth. Don't over mix. Use a spatula to scoop down sides and bottom of stand mixer - important step.

Cut out a circle of parchment paper for the bottom of a 10-inch cake pan. On the sides of the cake pan add butter and then a sprinkle of white flour emptying any excess. Place the parchment paper on the bottom.

Pour your ingredients into the pan and tap

onto the counter and smooth out the top with the back of a spoon. Thinly slice the remaining zucchini into tiny circles to place on the top. Add a little bit of olive oil to each circle, not too much and dab any excess.

Place in the oven to bake for roughly 1 hour and 10-15 minutes. It is done when a toothpick comes out dry and the outside is a deep golden brown. Let it sit on counter for 15 minutes. Then loosen the sides with a butter knife and carefully flip onto a cooling rack to cool for 30 minutes. (Who am I kidding — my family can never wait that long!) Enjoy!

Easy NY Style Bagels

YIELDS 11 SMALL BAGELS

This is an easy recipe to create delicious bagels that your family and friends will love! You do not have to let this dough rest overnight. And yes, most standard bagel recipes require bread flour, which is higher in protein and will produce a chewier bagel. I have tested this recipe many times and the result, using all-purpose flour, is still delicious.

Dough Ingredients:

3 ½ level cups all-purpose flour (extra for dusting)

1 packet rapid rise yeast, dissolved in ¼ cup warm water

4 tablespoons granulated sugar

1 ½ teaspoons table salt

1 ⅛ cups warm water, drizzle in while the mixer is on until dough forms.

Stand mixer with hook attachment

Other Ingredients:

A drizzle of a good quality extra virgin olive oil

1 tablespoon honey

2 baking sheets lined with parchment paper

Optional, 1 large egg, for egg wash

Everything bagel spices, or poppy and sesame seeds

Slotted spoon

Large, wide pot

Wood board

Pastry brush

Note: Rapid rise yeast works great for these easy and quick rise bagels, but an active dry yeast is equally as good. It may just take longer for the dough to double.

Preheat oven to 350 degrees.

First, dissolve the yeast packet in ¼ cup warm water. Give it a stir. Let it sit for 5 minutes. Transfer to the bowl of the stand mixer. Add in the sugar, flour, and salt and slowly drizzle in water as stand mixer is moving - a little at a time until dough forms together.

Then stop the mixer and roll onto a wood board lightly dusted with flour. Knead for 5-10 minutes. Let rest covered in a warm spot until it doubles roughly 1-1 ½ hours. Place on stovetop, after 30 minutes you may turn oven off.

Once dough doubles, punch down the dough and cover and let it rise for 10-15 minutes or longer until it slightly puffs again. Cut 11 equal size pieces using a kitchen shear. Shape into a ball by pulling all the dough downward toward the bottom, so seams are only at the bottom of the ball of dough.

Preheat oven to 425 degrees.

Next, roll the ball on the board, cupping it with one hand and using a repetitive, circular motion for 20 seconds or longer until a perfect ball has formed.

Put flour on your thumb and press a whole through the center of the ball and twirl on your index finger to stretch dough. You want to be sure you have a nicely rounded hole in the center, so you get that quintessential bagel shape. Cover the newly made bagels for 15 minutes — keep on the stovetop where it's warm, so they puff up.

Note: Sometimes the dough will stick to the parchment paper from the heat, so you may want to put down a very light dusting of flour under each bagel so that when you pick it up it keeps its shape and doesn't stick.

In the meantime, prepare the water bath. Bring a huge pot of water to a rapid boil. Be sure to add in 1 tablespoon (or more) of honey to brown the bagels. Turn down the heat a little and drop in 3 bagels (or more once you get the hang of it) at a time using a slotted spoon.

Important: They should float to the surface, then count 1 minute.

Then flip and count 1 more minute or slightly longer for a chewier bagel. Then flip back again to front side and transfer with a slotted spoon. Drain well over the pot of water. Place onto a baking sheet lined with parchment paper.

Bake for 19-20 minutes or until golden brown — turning the pan halfway through. Before they go in the oven is the time to mix 1 egg and brush on the egg wash and add the everything bagel seasoning to your bagels. You can do sesame or poppy or any seasoning you like. You may skip the egg wash altogether and just bake. The plain bagels you see in this photo are made without the use of an egg wash.

Have fun with the process! These will be a hit.

Note: If you are preparing these for your Chic Bagel Bar (page 27) do so a few hours before guests arrive. You may still want them warm, so leave a big pot with the water bath set up and have your baking sheets ready to go to boil the bagels. In the meantime, while dough is rising build your bagel board.

Cinnamon-Sugar Pretzels

YIELDS 8

Dough Ingredients:

4 cups all-purpose flour

1 cup 1% or 2 % milk, warmed

¼ warm water with 1 packet active dry yeast, dissolved

3 tablespoons light brown sugar

3 tablespoons salted butter, melted

2 teaspoons table salt

A good quality extra virgin olive oil

Stand mixer with hook attachment

Sugar-Cinnamon Coating:

½ stick salted butter, melted

½ cup granulated sugar

3 teaspoons cinnamon

Pastry brush

Paper bag for dusting pretzels

Water Bath:

10 cups water

½ cup baking soda

Large, wide pot

Slotted spoon

Whipped Cinnamon Cream Cheese Dipping Sauce:

⅓ cup heavy whipping cream

¼ cup cream cheese

½ teaspoon vanilla extract

1 tablespoon granulated sugar

A pinch of cinnamon-sugar mixture

Stand mixer with whisk attachment

Preheat oven to 350 degrees, so the stovetop is warm. This will give you a warm place to put the pretzel dough to rise. The pretzels bake at a much higher temperature.

Next, mix yeast into ¼ cup warm water and give it a stir. Let rest for 5 minutes. Then add to the bowl of the stand mixer. Combine the rest of the ingredients: milk, light brown sugar, melted butter, salt, and 4 cups all-purpose flour. Mix all the ingredients in the stand mixer until dough pulls away from sides of bowl. If it's a bit dry add in 1 tablespoon of water at a time.

Roll the dough onto a lightly floured clean work surface and knead for 5 minutes. Add the dough back into the stand mixer bowl, adding a drizzle of olive oil to bottom of bowl first and then to top of the dough. Cover and rest on back of stovetop. You can turn oven off once the stovetop seems warm. Let rise about 1 hour until doubled in size.

After 45 minutes, fill up a large pot with 10 cups of water and bring to a boil. Once dough has doubled, place the ball of dough onto the floured work surface and press into a large disc. Cut into ⅛ pieces. Roll each piece into a 20-inch rope, about ¾ inch thick.

In the meantime, preheat the oven to 450 degrees.

Now, shape the rope into a U. Take the ends and twist together twice then fold downward creating the classic pretzel shape. Once you have shaped the pretzels, check the water. Once it boils, turn it off then slowly add in the baking soda in ¼ cup at a time.

Then drop the pretzels in one at a time into the hot water for 20 to 30 seconds. If you go too long, they start to swell too much and then fall apart. Drop them gently into the water using a slotted spoon. I will flip them have way through, then turn back to top and take out.

After 20-30 seconds take out, drain over the pot and transfer to a baking sheet lined with parchment paper. You will need 2 baking sheets — 4 pretzels on each sheet. Let the pretzels rise a bit more. Let them air dry for a few minutes then cover for 5 minutes.

Next, place in the oven at 450 degrees for 11-12 minutes. Take out and brush with butter and sprinkle with sugar-cinnamon mixture or you can shake them in a bag to coat the entire pretzel.

If you prefer a savory pretzel, like Maggie, only use 1 tablespoon brown sugar in the dough. Then once they come out of the oven, brush with butter and add salt. You may also skip the butter and salt.

MAKING THE WHIPPED CINNAMON CREAM CHEESE DIPPING SAUCE:

In the bowl of a stand mixer with whisk attachment, whip the cream on high for 2 minutes. Add in the cream cheese and continue to whip on high for 2 more minutes. Next, add in the vanilla, cinnamon and sugar to taste. Whip until stiff peaks form. Place in a bowl with a pinch of cinnamon-sugar mixture on top.

Bits and Pieces

You are bits and pieces of all the women who came before you - your Mom, Grandma, aunts, sisters, and maybe even some teachers or mentors whose path you have crossed at some point in your life. Remember that you are intricately woven and uniquely created. All the women who came before you were part of your journey.

~ Trust Your Journey ~

Cakes and Cookies

Peach Pie
(Summertime)

SERVES 8

Growing up my mom hosted parties with her college friends "the gang" as she referred to them, and during the summer months, her friend would bring a homemade peach pie like this one. I never got the original recipe, but this is a close version. It is sweet with a hint of sour and the crust just melts in your mouth. If you are invited to a summer party bring this! It will not disappoint. It's even better on day 2.

Pie Crust Ingredients:

½ cup cold water

2 sticks cold salted butter, diced

2 ½ cups all-purpose flour (extra for dusting)

A pinch of table salt

3 tablespoons granulated sugar

Rolling pin

9 x 13 baking sheet

Food processor

Pie Filling Ingredients:

About ½ cup apricot jam

2-3 tablespoons granulated sugar

5-6 large firm peaches

Or 15 peach halves jarred (or canned)

Preheat oven to 400 degrees.

MAKING THE PIE CRUST:

In food processor add flour, a tiny pinch salt, sugar and pulse. Add diced butter and pulse a couple of times to break up the butter. (If you're doing by hand and using a pastry cutter, now is the time to hope you've been working your arms. Put some muscle into it!) Stream water into food processor and mix until the dough forms together. Add a tablespoon of water at a time as needed.

Note: If working it by hand, it may help to leave the butter on counter for 30 minutes before making dough. You may also make this in the stand mixer with hook attachment.

Once dough forms together, place onto a clean floured work surface. Work the dough with your hands until the butter is well incorporated throughout the dough.

With a rolling pin, shape the dough into a rectangle and press with your fingertips. The dough should be about ½-inch thick. Pinch all around the edges of the dough to create a little edge, so the juices do not leak off the sides. You may also crimp the edges and add more details

Transfer pie crust to a baking sheet lined with parchment paper. Alternatively, you may also shape it on the parchment paper, and then transfer to baking sheet. Refrigerate crust while you cut the peaches.

If you have a little excess dough you can make some star shapes using cooking cutter and add to one corner of the pie as a nice design element.

Wash and dry the peaches. Peel off the skin (or you may leave skin on) and thinly slice the peaches. They don't have to be perfect. It's hard to cut peaches because of the pit, so it can get a little messy and if they are really ripe, it's even more difficult.

In the meantime, add about half a jar of apricot jam to a tiny pot and heat it on low. Add in a few tablespoons of water and stir, turn off the heat and let it cool. Then toss the peaches into a clean bowl, pour in the cooled jam mixture and add a few tablespoons sugar and toss so that all the peach slices are covered.

Note: You may use peach halves in syrup which taste equally good. In this case, drain them and thinly cut. Do not add the sugar only the jam.

Remove pie crust from the fridge and pour the peaches onto the crust and spread with a spoon. You can arrange the slices any way you wish. Place pie in oven for roughly 55 minutes. It is done when the edges and bottom are a golden brown. Oven temperature can vary, so the first time you make it record the time.

Another idea is to cut jarred peach halves into thin slices and transfer each sliced half with a spatula to the pie crust and place down keeping all the slices together. In this case, brush on apricot jam mixture versus tossing. This looks more like French tart.

Lavender Infused Cheesecake

SERVES 8

In the summer, I make Lavender Infused Cheesecake when English Lavender is growing in abundance in my garden. I create a lavender simple syrup and pair with mascarpone cheese for a savory cheesecake. In the winter, I use the thyme simple syrup in lieu of the lavender syrup and combine with cream cheese – for a sweeter cheesecake. Either way, this is a delicious and creamy combination that your family and guests will love! I inherited a cheesecake making gene!

Ingredients:

16 ounces cottage cheese (4% fat content), room temperature

16 ounces mascarpone cheese, room temperature (or cream cheese)

¾ cup light sour cream, room temperature

3 tablespoons lavender syrup (or thyme syrup)

½ teaspoon pure vanilla extract

2 tablespoons all-purpose flour

1 cup granulated sugar

4 large whole eggs, room temperature

3 sage leaves or 5 thyme sprigs

Leave cheeses, sour cream and eggs out at room temperature for at least 1 hour

High-speed blender

Stand mixer with paddle attachment

9-inch spring form pan

Baking sheet lined with foil

Graham Cracker Crust:

2 cups graham cracker crumbs

1 stick salted butter, melted

¼ cup granulated sugar

2 sage leaves or 3 thyme sprigs, leaves only

2 teaspoons lavender syrup (or thyme syrup)

Lavender (or Thyme) Infused Simple Syrup:

1 cup water

1 cup granulated sugar

4 lavender flowers (or 4 thyme sprigs if making Thyme Infused Cheesecake)

MAKING THE LAVENDER SYRUP:

Stir together equal parts water and sugar. Bring to a boil, stir and let sugar dissolve. Stir until liquid is translucent. This creates a simple syrup, then you can infuse flavor. Take it off the burner, add in the lavender flowers (or thyme sprig) and give it a quick stir, and cover. Let steep until it's cool, strain, discard flowers (or sprigs) and then refrigerate. Use the lavender or thyme infused simple syrup for cocktails, cakes, cookies. Store in an air-tight container. You can use orange rind, or other garden herbs like rosemary or mint. Will last 1-2 weeks.

Note: If you are buying the lavender and not growing it in your yard, buy culinary lavender which is suitable for consumption while ornamental lavender is not.

MAKING THE GRAHAM CRACKER CRUST:

Preheat the oven to 350 degrees. Measure 2 cups of graham cracker crumbs and add to a high-speed blender. Next, pulse in 3 sage leaves (or the leaves from 3-4 thyme sprigs.) Pour this into a bowl. Add in the melted butter and 2 teaspoons lavender syrup (or thyme syrup) and mix until well incorporated. Mix by hand for 5 minutes.

Butter the bottom and sides of the spring form pan. Then press the crust inside the pan. Do your best to get the crumbs up the sides as high up as possible. Place the crust in the oven for 8-10 minutes. Then set this aside and let cool completely. Drop the oven temperature down to 325 degrees. Don't skip this step. Your crust will be perfect!

Next, prepare the filing. Rinse out the blender. Then add 16 ounces cottage cheese and pulse on high for 2 minutes until completely smooth. Next, using the stand mixer add in 16 ounces mascarpone and mix for 1-2 minutes

to make it creamy. Then transfer the cottage cheese from the blender to the stand mixer and combine with mascarpone cheese, mix for another minute. Be sure to use a spatula and scrape down the sides of the bowl. The mascarpone (and cream cheese) can clump.

Now add in 1 cup granulated sugar and mix until smooth. Then add in ½ teaspoon vanilla and 3 tablespoons of lavender syrup (or thyme syrup) and mix for 1 minute. Add 2 tablespoons of flour (my grandmother always did this) and mix, scrapping down the sides of the bowl to be sure it is all incorporated.

Add in ¾ cup of sour cream and mix until smooth — about 1 more minute. Add in 1 egg at a time until fully incorporated. Be sure not to overmix once the eggs are in because you will create air bubbles. If you see them, tap the spring form pan on the counter and use a spoon or fork to smooth out the top, some will pop when they come to the surface.

Note: Mix 1 egg at a time in a bowl with a fork, then add to mixer to reduce the chance of creating air bubbles. Sometimes if you trap too many air bubbles in your cheesecake it will puff up in the oven, but then drop and crack when you take it out. This has happened to me.

Reminder: Oven should be at 325 degrees. Place cake on a baking sheet lined with foil (in case the spring form pan leaks) and into the oven for about 1 hour and 20-25 minutes. Don't open the oven. One thing is for sure, cheesecakes do not like sudden temperature changes. Once cake has solidified and has puffed up a bit and turned a slight golden brown on edges, but the center is still slightly jiggly — you can take it out. If you feel it needs more time, add only 5 minutes at time. Or leave in the oven and turn it off for 10 minutes.

Let it cool 15-20 minutes then use a butter knife to detach sides from pan. Place on a cooling rack for 2 hours to cool. After 1 hour, release cheesecake from spring form pan, and allow it to continue to cool. Then place in refrigerator tightly covered.

Best served next day. It will keep for 3 days in the fridge. If you are freezing, place in freezer, uncovered for 45 minutes. Then wrap tightly in a freezer safe bag and place in freezer.

If your cake top is a little too brown or you have a few cracks, or you have air bubbles on the top of your cake — use a very thin layer of sour cream to thinly spread on top of the cake. It will make the cake appear pure white and fill in the cracks. Easy fix!

Be sure cake has sat at room temp for an hour after you take it out of the fridge. Let the sour cream soak in for 30 minutes to absorb. Works great and you will not taste the sour cream!

Garnish with blackberries or make blackberry-blueberry sauce to add to each slice. You can infuse more of the lavender syrup (or thyme syrup) into the sauce once it cools. It will be berry good!

Food for thought: In the event your cheesecake cracks, keep this in mind — in the ancient art of Kintsugi, they will fill cracked pottery with gold to highlight and accentuate the cracks. In this case, use an edible gold filling — it will be a fabulous conversation piece!

Our true beauty lies within our differences...

Date Pinwheels
with Toasted Sesame Seeds

YIELDS 35

I love to explore other cultures and learn about food history. I also really enjoy dates, and these cookies are my own spin on this Middle Eastern sweet treat – I have read about many different variations of this type of cookie.

I decided to layer the flavors by using a pumpkin seed paste AND a date paste. It's a yummy and creative combination that has a complex, aromatic taste thanks to the addition of fragrant cardamom spice. Try it both ways – combine the date paste with the pumpkin seed paste OR just add with the date paste filling – either way is so good! If you haven't experimented with cardamom spice go lightly. It's a very poignant spice.

These are delicious, fragrant and aromatic not too-sweet-cookies that will become popular in your home. I will make these and freeze them and take them out when I want a cookie. One of my favorites! These are a relatively healthy snack too.

Dough Ingredients:

Rolling pin
Stand mixer with hook attachment

3 ½ cups all-purpose flour

½ teaspoon table salt

1 packet active dry yeast, dissolved in ¼ cup warm water

¾ cup whole or 2% milk, warmed

1 stick salted butter, melted in microwave

¼ cup granulated sugar

2-3 yolks, for egg wash (large eggs)

Topping: Sesame seeds

Pastry board

Date Paste Filling:

2 packages pitted dates, about 35 dates

A pinch of cardamom spice

½ teaspoon ground cinnamon

3-4 tablespoons coconut oil

High-speed blender

Non-stick frying pan

Pumpkin Seed Paste:

1 cup roasted and salted pumpkin seeds, ground

⅛ teaspoon cinnamon

½ cup light brown sugar, packed

2 tablespoons coconut oil, warmed

Optional, a pinch of cardamom spice

High-speed blender

. . . .

MAKING THE DATE PASTE FILLING:
Soak dates in hot water for 5-10 minutes, then drain. Heat 3-4 tablespoons coconut oil in pan add the dates to gently warm. Then toss them into high-speed blender to create a paste and add back to the pan with the spices — a tiny pinch cardamom seasoning, ¼ teaspoon of cinnamon (or more). Heat on low for 1-2 minutes. Take off heat. Keep in pan to keep warm so it is easy to spread. Set this aside.

MAKING THE PUMPKIN SEED PASTE:
Pulse pumpkin seeds in blender add in sugar, cinnamon, dash cardamom, mix until all the seeds are ground into a powder-like consistency. Pour this mixture into a bowl. Next, heat 2 tablespoons of coconut oil in the microwave and mix into the mixture until you create a paste-like consistency. Set this aside.

MAKING THE DOUGH:
Measure ¼ cup warm water, add in one packet yeast, mix until it dissolves. Add to the bowl of the stand mixer and stir. Let sit for 5 minutes. It should resemble murky water and have some bubbles in it. After 5 minutes, add sugar, salt,

warmed milk, warmed butter, and flour. Using the hook attachment, mix until incorporated. The dough should come together quickly.

Place dough onto a clean floured work surface and knead for 5 minutes, using the palm of your hand. Then cover the dough and let it sit in a warm spot to double in size — 30 minutes or longer. I will typically turn on my oven and rest the dough inside the metal stand mixer bowl and place on the stovetop. The metal bowl will retain heat well and nudge allow the rising of the dough.

Cut the dough into seven pieces. Roll each piece into a ball and cover unused dough. Work with one ball of dough at a time. Roll the ball into a rectangle using a rolling pin. This dough should yield seven rectangles.

Working on a pastry board lightly dusted with flour, cut 6 by 10-inch rectangles using use a pastry cutter (or pizza cutter). Smear 3-4 heaping tablespoons of date paste and then layer 3 teaspoons of the pumpkin seed paste onto each rectangle using the back of a spoon or you may use a piece of parchment to evenly spread both mixtures onto the dough — highly recommended this to smooth out mixture.

Roll each dough sheet into a log and cut into 1-inch pieces — should yield 5 cookies per log. This makes roughly 35 cookies.

Place each cookie onto a baking sheet lined with parchment paper. Use a pastry brush to coat the dough with the egg yolk wash, and then add a good sprinkle of sesame seeds to each cookie.

Bake cookies in 2 separate batches at 350 degrees for 20 minutes — maybe a few minutes longer. Last minute or two, crank the oven to 375 (or higher) to get a blast of heat to make the top a golden-brown color. These puff up nicely in the oven. You will love these!

Chocolate Chickpea
Energy Bites

YIELDS 12

Ingredients:

2 ½ cups canned chickpeas, rinsed

½ cup almond butter

2 teaspoons vanilla

A dash of cinnamon

2 tablespoons whole oats

2 tablespoons honey

2 tablespoons cocoa powder, dark chocolate

Ground sea salt to taste

A handful of semi-sweet mini chocolate chips

1 bag sweetened coconut flakes, pulsed

Mini cupcake holders

A good quality extra virgin olive oil

Optional, mix flaxseed into batter
for added health benefits

Optional, 1 teaspoon freshly brewed coffee

These energy bites are very satisfying and tasty. Just one bite and you will be hooked and start making them every week like me. You will love these especially if you are a fitness enthusiast and want a sweet treat and a boost of energy. This is your new go-to sweet treat!

Start by pulsing 2 ½ cups of rinsed, canned chickpeas in a high-speed blender adding a slight drizzle of olive oil.

Next, add the chickpeas to a bowl along with the other ingredients: creamy almond butter (salted), vanilla extract, coffee (cooled), honey, cocoa powder (dark chocolate), a sprinkle of cinnamon, a few shakes of ground sea salt, and whole oats.

Mix these ingredients well, then add in a small handful of semi-sweet mini chocolate chips. If you find these are still too wet, add a bit more oats.

Place in the fridge for 20 minutes. Then roll into a ball. Cover them in coconut flakes.

Serve in a mini cupcake holder for easy eating. Store in the fridge for up to 5 days. You know they say you are what you eat, in this case, a ball of energy! Go get 'em!

Note: pulse the coconut flakes in the blender to break them up. This will make it easier to roll the balls.

Dark Chocolate Cake
with Jack's Fluffy Chocolate Icing

SERVES 8

This is an irresistible, super moist dark chocolate two-layer cake paired with a creamy, fluffy chocolate icing that Jack and I developed together. It has become a family favorite especially for special celebrations and holidays. This is my all-time favorite chocolate cake recipe which I have tested and retested many times. You will love this rich and delicious cake!

A few tips:

Don't pack the flour or cocoa powder. Simply spoon the flour and cocoa into the measuring cups and level off with a butter knife. I use dark chocolate cocoa powder for this recipe because it gives the cake a deep rich chocolatey flavor. Also, you will not taste the coffee whatsoever in this cake. It serves to enhance the flavor of the chocolate. You may omit and swap out with hot water. Remember it goes in last! Mix eggs separately, then add to stand mixer.

Ingredients:

1 ½ cups cake flour

1 ½ cups granulated sugar

¼ teaspoon baking powder

1 teaspoon baking soda

½ cup sour cream

¾ cup hot strong coffee

1 cup vegetable oil

¼ teaspoon table salt

1 tablespoon vanilla extract

¾ cup cocoa powder, dark chocolate

1 large egg

2 egg yolks

Two 8-inch rounds

Optional, egg substitute ½ cup apple sauce

Stand mixer with paddle attachment

Jack's Fluffy Chocolate Icing:

3 ½ cups powdered sugar

2 level tablespoons cocoa powder, dark chocolate

⅔ cup mascarpone (may substitute cream cheese)

2-3 tablespoons sour cream

1 tablespoon coffee, cooled

1 teaspoon vanilla

Stand mixer with whisk attachment

Preheat the oven to 350 degrees. Butter the sides of cake pans and lightly dust with all-purpose flour. Cut a circle of parchment paper for the bottom so the cake doesn't stick.

In a large bowl, whisk together the cake flour, dark chocolate cocoa powder, baking soda, baking powder and table salt. Set that aside.

In a stand mixer combine white sugar, vegetable oil, vanilla and sour cream. Separately mix eggs. Then add eggs to wet ingredients and mix. Next, add flour mixture and mix until well combined. Use a spatula to incorporate any batter on the sides and bottom of the bowl.

Last add in the hot coffee and mix until batter is lump free and smooth. Batter should be very liquidy! Use a strong, freshly brewed coffee for this recipe like an espresso Italian roast coffee.

Pour the batter into cake pans and tap on counter to release any air bubbles that have formed. Then place in oven. Let bake about 35 or more minutes until slightly springy.

Let cool on a cooling for 15 minutes, then loosen the sides with a butter knife and flip onto a cooling rack. Serve this with a little powdered sugar. Simple and delicious! Or top with Jack's Fluffy Chocolate Icing! Store-bought icing is great too.

MAKING JACK'S FLUFFY CHOCOLATE ICING:

Note: To achieve a creamy lighter and fluffier icing, add in at least 3 tablespoons sour cream. Use the whipping attachment on the stand mixer and whip for 2 minutes until you see the peaks forming. Keep adding powdered sugar as needed. You may loosen the icing with a tablespoon of milk if it is too thick. If you prefer a richer, darker chocolate icing you may omit the sour cream or use only 1 tablespoon, add milk as needed.

Place the mascarpone cheese in the stand mixer and whip. While it's moving add in 2-3 tablespoons sour cream. Mix these together.

Add in dark chocolate, cooled coffee and vanilla. Mix on high for 2 minutes. Periodically, stop the mixer and scrape down the sides and bottom of bowl with a rubber spatula.

Next, gradually add the powdered sugar in 2 parts. Keep the mixer moving until creamy and smooth and slightly increased in volume, 2-3 minutes. If it's runny add more powdered sugar. Mix until very fluffy and airy.

Amazing taste and you will NOT taste the sour cream! I hope you enjoy it as much as my family.

Note: If you are omitting the eggs and adding apple sauce — this is equally good and very moist. This is how I make it for Jack.

Storage: If not using immediately using the icing or you have some leftover icing, it can be refrigerated for up to 2 to 3 days in an airtight container. Before using, bring to room temperature and then beat until smooth again before using. Store cake in the refrigerator in an airtight container for up to 3 days.

Lemon and Poppy Seed Cookies
with Glaze

YIELDS 24

These are tangy, a little sweet, cakey and so good! In fact, they disappear in one day, so hide some for yourself. This recipe will yield about 2 dozen or more golf ball sized cookies. Feel free to load up on the lemon and lemon zest to make these extra tangy. Great for the holidays! This is an Italian classic cookie with a twist. The edible roses are added for a design element.

Ingredients:

2 level cups all-purpose flour

½ cup mascarpone cheese, room temperature

½ cup light cream cheese, room temperature

1 stick salted butter, softened

¼ teaspoon vanilla extract

½ teaspoon baking soda

½ teaspoon baking powder

½ cup white granulated sugar

Zest of 1 large lemon

1 large lemon squeezed

Optional, 1 teaspoon poppy seeds (or more) and edible dried roses

Stand mixer with paddle attachment

Glaze:

2 ¼ cups powdered sugar

⅓ cup milk

½ lemon squeezed

Zest of ½ lemon

Preheat oven to 350 degrees. Line a baking sheet with parchment paper.

In a stand mixer, add in the softened butter. If your butter is cold, put it in a microwave safe bowl and in the microwave for 20 seconds or less to slightly warm it.

Next, mix the butter for 2 minutes on a low setting until creamy. Then add mascarpone and cream cheese to the mixer and mix until the butter and cheeses have combined and become smooth, about 2-3 minutes.

Next, add in sugar and mix for a minute. Add in vanilla, lemon zest, and 1 lemon

158

HEART & HOME

squeezed. Scrape down sides of bowl to fully incorporate the wet ingredients.

In a medium-sized bowl, add flour, baking soda, baking powder, salt, and poppy seeds. Whisk the dry ingredients. Mix until combined.

Then add the dry ingredients to the wet ingredients in stages. It will form into a sticky dough. If it's a too sticky, add a tablespoon of flour. It's a cakey cookie, so the little extra flour, will not impact the texture of the cookie.

Using a spoon, scoop up a 1-inch ball of dough and place on a baking sheet lined with parchment paper — 3 across and 4 down. You can shape it into a ball by putting some flour on your hands if the dough is too sticky.

Place in the oven about 14-15 minutes until they are firm, and the bottom is a golden brown. Don't over bake.

Once cookies are done, place on a cooling rack. Let cool 30 minutes. Dip in the glaze and fully cover the cookie, and let it set at room temperature. Then store cookies in an airtight container.

MAKING THE GLAZE:

In a small mixing bowl whisk together powdered sugar, lemon zest, half of a lemon squeezed, and milk and whisk until smooth. You may use the stand mixer as well. The icing should be on the thicker side, and no lumps. It should be pure white with specks of lemon zest popping through.

Lay down a piece of parchment paper under the cooling rack and dip the top of each cookie, covering all the nooks and crannies. You may dip twice.

Let the icing set completely, once hardened and they are ready to eat! Store in an air-tight container for 3-4 days. Can freeze as well.

CHAPTER 9

My Faith Journey

The best ingredient is Confidence
The best nutrient is Love

Faith has always been an important part of my life. Part of my faith includes believing that we are all led on our faith journey, and in fact, I was literally led to the homeless shelter to volunteer. Let me explain.

In 2015, I started my blog. My goal all along was to write a cookbook documenting and preserving my family's recipes and share recipes from my own kitchen that my family loved. This became my life's passion — cooking was something I loved to do for my family — it was also a means of survival in the case of feeding Jack. Cooking has always been my way of showing my family how much I love and care for them. I had developed a gift of creativity in the kitchen, but what good is a gift if you don't share it?

Soon after I published my first cookbook, *Mariooch's Kitchen Food That Will Gather Your Family*, I felt it was important to share my talent in a more hands-on way.

For many years, I prepared warm lunches on a rotation schedule for a local preschool where many of the children were homeless. Once the school closed, I began looking for a way to volunteer my time. I heard about a homeless shelter that was about twenty-five minutes away. I was hesitant to drive that far. Getting on the highway with fast-moving trucks wasn't something I wanted to do either. I cringe when I share the road with large, fast trucks.

God had another plan...

The homeless shelter kept coming up because our local community does a lot to support this organization, so I was encouraged by my husband to set up a date to meet with the director, see and inspect the kitchen, and decide what I would do after that. After meeting with the director, I knew it was the right fit.

On the day that I was scheduled to volunteer in the teaching kitchen, I said a quick prayer as I was about to enter the highway: "God, please clear my path from big trucks."

By the way, did I mention I drive a huge pick-up truck?

As I entered the road, there was not a truck in sight...and as I have made the journey to teach in the kitchen over the past two years, there have been barely any trucks (at least much bigger than mine) in my path. I was literally led to the homeless shelter to share my talents as a chef...It still amazes me.

I don't think of it as volunteering — it's more like being part of a community of mainly women. The bonds that these women share and the love and support they have for each other is remarkable. I walk in and see them feeding or holding their friend's baby, laughing and joking with each other. It is heartwarming.

Every time the babies come in, I want to hold and feed them myself — and I do, as do my kids when they come with me. This way the moms can do the cooking and feel a sense of pride and self-satisfaction in taking part in creating the meal.

Homelessness can happen to anyone. I am so happy to be a volunteer chef, but more importantly hope that through my influence I may in some small way change the trajectory of someone's life. I think everyone who volunteers at the shelter feels this way...we mentor through our conversations, through our example, and through our true concern for the residents' well-being. I do my best to initiate conversations in the kitchen — some talking about the choices we make and how that can lead us down the wrong path. Sometimes we talk about getting a job in the food industry because some of women are good in the kitchen.

The career development staff found a job for one of the women after I alerted them that this client was formerly a chef and is impressive in the kitchen. It was a great day when I heard she was employed!

More recently, after we prepped a meal and before everyone sat at the table to eat, I asked if everyone would like to say a prayer — I think holding onto faith and keeping that as a source of peace and hope is important. It's a necessary and comforting resource.

Here's one prayer which I led: "Be stronger than your circumstances. Know that God is always beside you and in times like these He carries you."

Poverty alleviation has been important to me from the time I walked, as a teacher, into the doors of an elementary school where some of the kids were poor. A few kids would come in hungry.

It was important to me through the years to help alleviate poverty. Being a part of this community has given me this opportunity to make a difference. However, every time I drive away from the shelter I cry.

I cry because I don't want to see that mom with the baby feeling sad. I cry because it's sad to think that some of these women have family in the area who won't take them in. I cry because someone is disabled and can't work and can't pay her bills and has no choice but to be there. I genuinely believe that when one person hurts, we all hurt — this is my life's philosophy. Maybe our world would be a better place if we could all think like this.

On the flip side, I also laugh so hard that

I cry, like when I meet a guest in the kitchen whose name I want to remember and he says, "Remember these three famous athletes all starting with the name Michael?" Ah-ha! His name is Michael and I will never forget him and his tall stature. Michael taught me how to grill tortillas on the stovetop — as I stood close by with the fire extinguisher. Ha-ha! Thank you, Michael!

The men are very funny, and it's so wonderful how they too want to be hands-on in the kitchen. They tell the best stories, too. One guest talked about how his grandmother would say, "Everyone's going to be hungry and if your wife comes home and she is tired, you have to learn how to make a meal to feed everybody." Smart woman!

We take it one conversation at a time... some impactful, some basic chatting; one meal at a time...all yummy, healthy, and affordable; one day at a time in the hopes of a brighter future.

Here are some money saving tips I'd like to share:

- Mash white beans into ground beef or turkey. No one will know they are in there, and it will provide essential nutrients and vitamins and stretch the meat.

- Purée white beans into cheese sauces. White beans have a neutral taste that no one will recognize but it will develop a creamy sauce to toss over pasta, eliminating some of the cheese which can be high in fat and expensive. You can do the same with puréed cauliflower.

- Add puréed yams into sauces combined with cheese for a nutritious boost

that is creamy and undeniably good. Or try puréed butternut squash combined with cheese to increase the nutritional profile of a pasta meal.

- Substitute pasta for whole wheat pasta, lentil or chickpea pastas.

We have made:

Homemade ravioli and pasta

Homemade pizza

Healthy Macaroni and cheese

Vegetarian tacos

Other vegetarian meals

Snickerdoodle cookies made with yams

Guacamole using broccoli stems

Chicken soup

And much, much more

About the Author

Mary is an author of multiple books, and an entrepreneur promoting her brand "Mariooch's Kitchen". She lives amidst horse and fresh produce farms in a scenic suburban town with her husband Peter and their children Maggie, Sydney, and Jack. A talented chef and accomplished food stylist and photographer, Mary inherits her love of cooking from her Italian grandmother. Mariooch "little Mary" in Italian was a fitting choice for her brand as it was a nickname given to her by her Italian Father. Mary meticulously adapts recipes to preserve old-world flavor and heritage while updating recipes to fit her family's taste and healthy lifestyle. She also loves exploring other cultures in her new cookbook. It offers many healthy recipes with creative twists and is jammed packed with entertaining tips and styling ideas.

Prior to turning her attention full-time to growing "Mariooch's Kitchen," Mary earned her MBA. When she's not busy cooking, entertaining or blogging, Mary enjoys long walks outdoors, watching her children's myriad of activities including watching her daughter Sydney pole vault, and beach get-a-ways. Her hidden talent is hitting the speed bag, which she considers akin to life and says, "Timing is everything."

"Guard, honor and cherish the family dinner," she says.

Index

Recipe Index

Made in the USA
Middletown, DE
09 March 2021